The RE

H...BOOK

Available from Continuum

100 Ideas for Teaching English -- Angella Cooze
100 Ideas for Teaching Religious Education – Cavan Wood
Teaching English 3-11 – Cathy Burnett and Julia Myers
Getting the Buggers to Write: 2nd Edition – Sue Cowley
Getting the Buggers to Read: 2nd Edition – Claire Senior
Encouraging Reading – Susan Elkin

The Handbook Series

The Citizenship Teacher's Handbook – Kate Brown and Stephen Fairbrass
The Mathematics Teacher's Handbook – Mike Ollerton
The Trainee Teacher's Secondary Handbook – Gererd Dixie

The RE Teacher's Handbook

Cavan Wood

continuum

Continuum Internatinoal Publishing Group

The Tower Building	80 Maiden Lane, Suite 704
11 York Road	New York,
SE1 7NX	NY 10038

www.continuumbooks.com

Main text © Cavan Wood 2009

British Library Cataloguing-in-Publication Data
A catalogue record for this book is available from the British Library.

Library of Congress Cataloging-in-Publication Data
Wood, Cavan
  The RE teacher's handbook / Cavan Wood
    p.   cm.
  Includes index.
  ISBN 978-1-84706-385-4
  1. Religion–Study and teaching–Great Britain.   2. Religious–Study and teaching–
Great Britain.   I. Title.   II. Title: Religious education teacher's handbook.

  BL41.W576 2009
  200.71'041–dc22

                                                                    2008048121

Typeset by BookEns Ltd, Royston, Herts.
Printed in Great Britain by the MPG Books Group, Bodmin and King's Lynn

Contents

Introduction

Get 25 new views on the meanings of life. Teach RE. Children's views are always fresh – just imagine how stimulating they'll be on the really big questions. RE teachers come from a variety of backgrounds: your degree doesn't have to be in religious education. Use your head. Teach.
An advert from the Teacher Training Agency, 2005

This was one of the first occasions on which recruitment of teachers had been targeted at potential RE teachers. So, is the experience of teaching RE as rich as the advert suggests? It certainly can be. Spending time thinking through those big – or more correctly, ultimate – questions is an enormous privilege. To help pupils begin to articulate their moral and spiritual opinions can be very rewarding.

Yet, to be an RE teacher, you may well need an inner strength. Your English or Maths colleagues seldom get the question, 'What's the point of doing this subject?' You will. There is a need to be able to give an explanation of the importance of the subject in language that can be understood by pupils in both Key Stages 3 and 4. So what would you say? There are times when the suffering servant of Isaiah seems to be a good image for the RE Teacher – despised and rejected by all. We have been described on occasion as 'the Cinderella subject'. The job of the RE teacher is to make sure the subject becomes a princess – in the Middle Ages, theology was 'the queen of sciences' after all!

A Christian friend of mine once said, 'I have never understood why Jesus talked about casting pearl before swine'. On those bad, grey and rainy days in November, when you have a non-exam group who seem to be sitting though a lesson with real resentment, then you might understand, I told him!

The religious traditions, their stories and their teachings are pearls that we should try to share with the pupils we teach. We are opening a vast treasury of ideas that will help pupils to develop their own thinking and understanding. The responsibility to get it right is enormous and we should not take it lightly. Consider this – the parable of Tavistock Square:

> Across the road from Euston Station is Tavistock Square. It was here on July 7th 2005 that a young Muslim man blew himself up on a double decker bus. Immediately opposite where this happened is Tavistock Square park. There is a statue of Gandhi which sits in the park. In another corner, there is a tribute to those who were conscientious objectors to the world wars. There is a stone erected to remember the dead of Hiroshima. The park has the names of people who are Humanist, Jewish, Hindu, Sikh, Christian – the park is the whole community of Britain in a single space.

The park was set up for peace and yet a terrible crime happened just outside its border.

Religion, too, should bring peace but, too often, there have been terrible crimes at its border. Our job as educators should be to challenge, to bring the spirit of the people who set up Tavistock Park into being. I found peace in Tavistock Square, even though I could have just been reminded of cruelty and violence.

C.S. Lewis once wrote that he wanted to help himself from a false image of himself, of others and of God. That seems a good curriculum aim, doesn't it? Encouraging students to reflect on these is an important part of their development and will influence many generations.

I hope that this book will help to equip you for your role as a teacher of RE. I had thought about calling it 'Everything you wanted to know about teaching RE but were afraid to ask'. I hope that whether you are a trainee, an NQT or an established Head of Department, you will find something here to help you to do your job better.

Cavan Wood

The evolution of Religious Education

Since I was a pupil in the 1970s, the subject I teach has variously been called the following:

- Religious Instruction
- Religious Knowledge
- Religious Education
- Religious Studies

Each title revealed some of the assumptions that the teachers brought to it. Religious Instruction suggested not just the imparting of knowledge, but giving instruction in order to change behaviour and beliefs. It was the time of moral absolutes, or at least the attempt to make pupils believe they were still in force.

Religious Knowledge wanted to focus on the acquiring of facts. The two titles most used now are Religious Education and Religious Studies. The 'Education' title seems to be most used when describing teaching that is not necessarily motivated by exams, with 'Religious Studies' being linked with examinations. Sometimes, RE is often confused with the spiritual component offered by collective worship. Although assemblies should be educational, they are not essentially RE.

In Scotland, the subject is known as Religious and Moral Education. At times, there is a movement to re-name the subject. I know of one school that refers to it as 'Quest', trying to take it away from using the word 'religious'. There can be embarrassment at the title 'Religious' but we cannot and should not avoid this. Anyway, with a curriculum as we have it, pupils will soon work out what the content of the subject really is, whatever we might choose to call it!

Yet, it remains a fact that both the short and the long courses in RE/RS are some of the fastest growing subjects in the curriculum. Schools are beginning to wake up to the fact that they need to deliver RE in a way that both engages and potentially rewards students.

For ease, let us call it RE. The content of RE has changed, as well as its name. In the 1940s, it was exclusively a study of the Bible, with some church history added in. By the late 1950s, this was becoming increasingly difficult to sustain. Students were openly rebelling against the subject and it was left to two researchers to think the way forward. Something had to change.

Following the research of Harold Loukes, schools began to develop a focus on the moral and spiritual questions of teenagers. (Effectively, this led to the development of Personal and Social Education as we know it.) These questions could still be used to engage with the Biblical texts to help students see the Bible's relevance to their world. There were others who questioned whether teenagers could make such connections to the Bible and the modern world. Was it too remote and obscure to be relevant?

The work of Ronald Goldman questioned whether pupils could handle the Bible anyway, for, as he pointed out, 'The Bible is not a children's book'. Yet, RE often seemed to treat it as such. The image of Jesus was far from the radical, demanding prophet – more an extension of the 'gentle Jesus, meek and mild' of Sunday School.

By the beginning of the 1970s, the large-scale immigration of people of other faiths meant that other cultures and religions were suddenly brought into sharp focus. There was an increasing interest in what was called 'Comparative religion', in which other faiths were explained often on the basis of how they compared, matched or diverged from Christianity. Yet this became unpopular, as people reflected that you should not compare religions, but seek to understand them within their own terms. Salvation might be a key term in Christianity but it is an irrelevant concept to agnostic Buddhism, more interested in gaining enlightenment. Increasingly, world religions were taught and written into syllabuses. Many schools only chose to study the religions that their members of staff could understand: as the majority of RE teachers in the 1970s had Christian roots or understanding, Islam and Judaism were often taught in preference to the religions of the East, Hinduism, Sikhism and Buddhism. Gradually, as the universities broadened their teaching to include more on world religions in either Theology or Religious Studies courses, more teachers were prepared to look at all the major world religions.

As the 1970s came to an end, the pattern of RE was becoming a combination of Christianity, a study of a topic across religions such as pilgrimage or life after death and the study of world religions. The teaching of world religions was often a bit of a shock to many teachers who had perhaps begun to teach RE in order to share their views on Christianity. When I was taught about world religions in the mid-1970s, my school allocated half-term modules to explain to me the rudiments of Buddhism, Islam, Judaism, Sikhism and Hinduism: it reminds me of that Monty Python sketch about summarizing Proust in a sentence and about as successful! This meant the teaching was, by its very nature, both superficial and confusing.

This confusion was later addressed by the locally agreed syllabuses that instructed teachers to make sure that they taught Christianity and two other world religions at each Key Stage in depth and not try to deliver all of them in a rush. What mattered was breadth and depth, not either/or.

One key document that began to set the changes in RE was the 1975 Birmingham syllabus, which included not just religious ideas, but also Communism. This reflected the thinking of Ninian Smart, who felt that you could study Communism as if it were religious. After all, they had sacred books, charismatic leaders, an idea of a utopian and an asset of demonic-like enemies that are opposed to their world view. It also had a kind of eschatology, albeit dependant on the working class seeing their destiny to replace the cruel rich. Increasingly, there was a sense of responsibility to look at atheist or agnostic beliefs like Humanism to show pupils the complexity of human belief.

In the 1980s, the position of RE seemed under threat. It was not part of the core or statutory curriculum, but part of the basic curriculum. This was often ill-defined and did lead to some pressure on the subject, despite the provision in law since 1944 that it had to be taught. When the Dearing Report in the National Curriculum was published in the 1990s, he recommended that RE should have 5 per cent of curriculum time. With the development of the Short Course RE GCSE, it became increasingly easy to support the development or the maintenance of the subject to governors, staff, pupils and parents. Even on an hour a week, a student could now be rewarded for the hard work in RE, rather than see it as wasted time, as it was not going to lead to any qualification.

Yet, there were still issues to tackle. Many favoured the replacement of RE with Citizenship, but the practical nature of schools has meant that, in many schools, Citizenship was seen as a subject that seemed to be in part a development of the moral and social education, as well as RE being given to the RE department in order to somehow develop within the school.

RE is a subject that is constantly evolving. In the 1990s, the faith communities were asked to help to draw up model syllabuses of what they thought a well informed pupil should know about their faith. These have proved to be very influential in the development of textbooks, exam content, as well as the local syllabuses. They encouraged the development of the emphasis of learning about (i.e. developing knowledge of the faith) and learning from (i.e. developing their own opinions, using the faith input) faith.

The 1980s also saw an attempt to think about more active approaches to RE, pioneered as a result of the research that David Hay had undertaken in the 1970s. This experiential RE encouraged meditation, guided fantasy and role-play amongst other techniques in order to bridge the increasing sense of divide between the majority of pupils' lack of experience of religion and the subject content. It was hoped that this would be able to restore relevance to a world that seemed either secular or confusingly multicultural. These would offer experiences like religious ones, so that RE students with a secular background should have an opportunity to develop empathy.

There were other strands, too. Writers like Robert Kirkwood, in his series of books such as *Looking for God* (Robert Kirkwood, Longman, 1988), tried to make religious language and philosophy open to the understanding of even the youngest members of a secondary school. Their use of cartoon drawings and minimum text seemed much more preferable and more suited to mixed-ability classes than the somewhat wordy and worthy books on comparative religion or Biblical studies that preceded them. Kirkwood and, more recently, writers like Dwilyn Hunt have tried to encourage pupils to think about higher-level questions in language that is appropriate to the age range. RE became less about drawing a map of Sumeria or naming the five Ks and more about ideas.

Undoubtedly, the rise of phemenonlogy of religion in such books as Ninian Smart's *The Religious Experience of Mankind* (Fount, 1980) greatly influenced RE. Descriptions of rituals and their meanings to believers became very important. The externals of religion were thoroughly studied, but this often meant that the real meaning behind what was going on was obscured.

People were encouraged to bracket out their feelings or faith to make objective descriptions of what is going on in religion. Others saw RE as helping to track groups, such as the approach of Professor Robert Jackson, based on ethnographic approaches, in which religious communities were tracked over time.

There have many different streams that have fed into the river of the subject: we should learn to value them all and to learn from each. We need to make sure that our students have a flavour of all of these different ways of seeing, as this will enable them to see the multifaceted nature of the truth of the religious experience.

Yet, still we might encounter this problem, as the following case study shows. How do you react to this?

Case study: What's the point of RE?

Dawn has a class that includes a pupil who frequently asks why they have to do RE. 'None of us are going to be vicars. Why do we need your subject?' the pupil says. The class is a non-exam class, Key Stage 4. You think that they need some reward for studying, perhaps for a Short Course GCSE.

Should she try to explain why RE is studied in the lesson or should she have a discussion with the pupil outside of the classroom? Should Dawn encourage her reluctant Head of Department (who only teaches brighter pupils at Key Stage 4) to think about adopting the Short Course GCSE?

We need to be able to develop clear, pupil-friendly responses to this challenge. We need to help them to see that it is about the development of them as people, not just about their understanding of what might appear to them to be relevant. This is a subject that has more relevance than some students often appreciate. Key to forming an answer is the emphasis on the spiritual and their need to be prepared for the multicultural and multi-religious nature of the world we live in. Yet, we also need to be able to offer a pragmatic approach as well.

Pupils do respond best to courses from which they can see some reward. If it is possible, some type of certification is much more likely to help pupils. This will give them a focus and a purpose. At the very least, some internal certification could be put into pupil profiles. However, how well has the department articulated to the students the importance of RE? One of the earliest things teachers should do with students is to look at the importance of the subject and to re-enforce this by making sure that there is a good balance between learning about and learning from religion, so that the relevance of the subject is constantly explored.

What follows is the QCA justification for RE: think about the issues it raises and how its points could be communicated to students and their parents.

QCA on the importance of religious education

Successful learners
RE helps to develop successful learners by asking life's largest questions and presenting interesting, important conceptual challenges to pupils. Learning about religion and learning from religion has the capacity to motivate and empower pupils, enabling them to enjoy and value learning.

By investigating beliefs and teachings, explaining practices, reflecting on questions of truth, analysing ideas and evaluating answers, pupils can enhance their skills and confidence as learners. Pupils engage with spiritual and moral concepts, some of which may be new to them, by reflecting on, analysing, interpreting and evaluating sources, questions, practices or ideas. Understanding the complexity of questions about truth, meaning, purpose, identity, values or commitments, and analysing possible answers, can contribute to successful learning individually and collaboratively.

As pupils interpret sources and texts with increasing skill, they begin to ask questions about truth and meaning, and to understand the importance of communicating ideas accurately and respectfully. Applying vocabulary, explaining commitments, and evaluating beliefs enhance pupils' skills and confidence as group learners as they work with others to give expression to their understanding and response.

Confident individuals
RE helps to create confident individuals by promoting self-awareness and self-esteem as pupils articulate questions and explore responsibility. RE provides a forum for young people to voice their questions about identity and meaning, contributing to their personal development. It can inspire pupils to search for and deepen their sense of personal meaning in their lives. As young people reflect on ultimate questions and on the ideas and

practices of belief systems, they are helped to understand more about themselves and others, and how to communicate. They are encouraged to develop their ideas and express them appropriately. They can use beliefs, practices and values to deal confidently with challenges and setbacks. Evaluating practices, ways of life and values empowers pupils to make informed choices. They learn to take increasing responsibility for their attitudes and actions.

These processes also strengthen pupils' realistic confidence in themselves and each other, and help them to make decisions with increasing autonomy and discernment. This enables them to deal with the demands of adult life sensitively and competently.

Responsible citizens

RE helps prepare pupils to become responsible citizens by raising issues of local, national and global concern and placing them in spiritual and moral contexts. By understanding the beliefs and practices of religions and world views, pupils can make connections between belief and action. Through considering the beliefs behind environmental action, the needs of refugees or the work of aid agencies, pupils can become aware of the connections between beliefs, lifestyles and ultimate questions.

Understanding the right to hold different beliefs enables pupils to see diverse religions and beliefs as a significant part of the local, national and global community, and of human experience. They can develop as reflective and responsible citizens in a plural society and global community, with a strong awareness of religious and ethical diversity. By evaluating ethical issues, and expressing views using reasoned arguments, pupils can enhance their capacity and desire to make a positive contribution to debates and decisions.

Successful learners

RE helps to develop successful learners by asking life's largest questions and presenting interesting, important conceptual challenges to pupils. Learning about religion and learning from religion has the capacity to motivate and empower pupils, enabling them to enjoy and value learning.

By investigating beliefs and teachings, explaining practices, reflecting on questions of truth, analysing ideas and evaluating answers, pupils can enhance their skills and confidence as learners. Pupils are able to engage with spiritual and moral concepts, some of which may be new to them, by reflecting on, analysing, interpreting and evaluating sources, questions, practices or ideas.

Understanding the complexity of questions about truth, meaning, purpose, identity, values or commitments, and analysing possible answers, can contribute to successful learning individually and collaboratively.

As pupils interpret sources and texts with increasing skill, they begin to ask questions about truth and meaning, and to understand the importance of communicating ideas accurately and respectfully. Applying vocabulary, explaining commitments, and evaluating beliefs enhance pupils' skills and confidence as group learners as they work with others to give expression to their understanding and response.

Confident individuals

RE helps to create confident individuals by promoting self-awareness and self-esteem as pupils articulate questions and explore responsibility. RE provides a forum for young people to voice their questions about identity and meaning, contributing to their personal development. It can inspire pupils to search for and deepen their sense of personal meaning in their lives. As young people reflect on ultimate questions and on the ideas and practices of belief systems, they are helped to understand more about themselves and others, and how to communicate. They are encouraged to develop their ideas and express them appropriately. They can use beliefs, practices and values to deal confidently with challenges and setbacks. Evaluating practices, ways of life and values empowers pupils to make informed choices. They learn to take increasing responsibility for their attitudes and actions.

These processes also strengthen pupils' realistic confidence in themselves and each other, and help them to make decisions with increasing autonomy and discernment. This enables them to deal with the demands of adult life sensitively and competently.

Responsible citizens

RE helps prepare pupils to become responsible citizens by raising issues of local, national and global concern and placing them in spiritual and moral contexts. By understanding the beliefs and practices of religions and world views, pupils can make connections between belief and action. Through considering the beliefs behind environmental action, the needs of refugees or the work of aid agencies, pupils can become aware of the connections between beliefs, lifestyles and ultimate questions. Understanding the right to hold different beliefs enables pupils to see diverse religions and beliefs as a significant part of the local, national and global community, and of human experience. They can develop as reflective and responsible citizens in a plural society and global community, with a strong awareness of religious and ethical diversity. By evaluating ethical issues, and expressing views using reasoned arguments, pupils can enhance their capacity and desire to make a positive contribution to debates and decisions in society.

(QCA website, 2008)

Teaching and learning

Key Stage 3 RE

Any thinking about the content of RE has to reflect on a number of sources and issues. We, like colleagues in other subjects, start from where the whole curriculum has got to and then try to think about the place of RE within that whole. RE was given the status of being part of the Basic Curriculum, with the Dearing Report of the 1990s suggesting that this entitled RE to the equivalent of 5 per cent of time. Yet, we are also working in a time at which the curriculum is loosening and working with other subjects is becoming increasingly on the agenda again, in a way that it has not since the late 1970s.

What are the aims of the National Curriculum now?

The National Curriculum, as revised for September 2008, says the following:

> The curriculum should enable all young people to become:
>
> - successful learners who enjoy learning, make progress and achieve
> - confident individuals who are able to live safe, healthy and fulfilling lives
> - responsible citizens who make a positive contribution to society.

The new curriculum encourages the development of values, of community and of being self-confident in their own beliefs as well as others'. Students are to 'appreciate the benefits of diversity'. They need to be aware of human rights and live at peace with others. They need to have an understanding of the culture and traditions of others as well as their own.

Having the aims of the curriculum either in your teaching file or on display in your classroom will be good to help you deal with students who cannot see the immediate use of RE. It is all there – spelt out eloquently in that document. See it in detail at www.qca.co.uk.

RE developed for both Key Stages 3 and 4 must look to other areas as well. The local as well as the national situation will influence what we do at the Key Stages, especially the influence of the local SACRE.

The work of a SACRE

SACRE stands for the Standing Advisory Council on Religious Education and is a committee of your local authority. Since 1988, every local education authority has had to set up a SACRE to advise and monitor the delivery of RE in your area. Every SACRE has four committees:

1. Committee A consists of members of the main Christian churches and other religions. These should reflect the religious traditions in the area.
2. Committee B is made up of Church of England representatives.
3. Committee C is made up of teachers, often chosen from teacher associations or unions.
4. Committee D consists of representatives of the local education authority, which represent the political groupings on the council.

Each of these committees has equal voting rights when it comes to implementing reform or development of its work. Committees meet usually three times a term, though a small steering group may meet more frequently in order to prepare documentation and ideas for the other committees. Some SACREs have also been involved in the monitoring of teacher training in RE in their area.

The SACRE should give advice on RE, especially the locally agreed syllabus and the issue of collective worship. It is responsible for updating the locally agreed syllabus every 5 years, so that it reflects good practice in RE and the changes that may have occurred in the area.

SACREs have been praised by both OFSTED and HMI for helping to develop community cohesion and understanding.

Many SACREs have adopted the QCA's 2004 document 'The Non-Statutory National Framework For Religious Education' to help them to re-write their local agreed syllabus, as this is increasingly seen as a way for consistency to be developed across the subject and the different LEAs.

The 151 SACREs all belong to the National Association of SACREs, which seeks to help with the national co-ordination of the local bodies, so that they can share good practice and lobby for mutual concerns.

Try to find your local member of the SACRE, so that you can share your concerns. Ask your LEA for a list of members. You might even want to think about joining this group and influencing the development of the subject.

The non-statutory schemes of work

Increasingly, SACREs are drawing on the material offered to them as possibilities from the QCA. This may mean that we will eventually have a national syllabus.

The model schemes of work from the QCA do offer a selection of topics that can be incorporated into Key Stage 3. They were originally designed to provide material for six-week modules in Key Stage 3, leaving some of the content of the year to the local situation of the school, requirements of the locally agreed syllabus and the specialities that particular RE departments might possess. These topics originally included the following:

> Unit 7A. Where do we look for God? This unit looks at the ideas people
>   have about God and how they have tried to seek him.
> Unit 7B. What does justice mean to Christians? This looks at Biblical and
>   other Christian ideas that influence ideas.
> Unit 7C. Religious figure (generic) . This gives a scheme that collects a
>   series of questions and approaches that can be applied to any
>   religious leader/founder.
> Unit 7D. Who was Gotama Buddha? This enables students to reflect on
>   the life and teaching of the Buddha.
> Unit 7E. What are we doing to the environment? This looks at a number
>   of different religions and their approaches to dealing with the issues
>   about the care of the Earth and animals.
> Unit 8A. What does Jesus' incarnation mean for Christians today? This
>   encourages students to look at the differences in the Christmas
>   stories.

Unit 8B. What does the Resurrection of Jesus mean for Christians today? This encourages students to think through the theological ideas around the Resurrection, asking students to think about evidence that Christians present.

Unit 8C. Beliefs and practice (generic) . This sets out some ideas that could be applied to several world faiths that have been agreed in the local syllabus.

Unit 8D. Beliefs and practice: how do the beliefs of Sikhs affect their actions?

Unit 8E. A visit to a place of worship (generic) . This gives a framework that can be applied to any religion.

Unit 8F. What makes a gurdwara special to Sikhs? This develops the above scheme by specifying the Sikh holy place.

Unit 9A. Where are we going? Rites of passage. These look at the importance of ceremonies.

Unit 9B. Where did the universe come from? This looks at the ideas of science and the power of creation stories to be able to move and explain complex ideas.

Unit 9C. Why do we suffer? This looks at the big questions of suffering and evil.

Unit 9D. Why are some places special to religious believers? This looks at some key places – including the role of Jerusalem in Jewish, Christian and Islamic traditions.

In 2007, the QCA suggested the following additions to the model schemes:

Year 7 How can beliefs and values serve as a guide for moral decision making? This has been designed to show students how important religious beliefs can be in making oral decisions and is attempting to cement into the Key Stage 3 RE schemes of work that have traditionally been the province of GCSE or Key Stage 4.

Year 8 How do people express their spirituality through the creative arts? Using Buddhism, Christianity, Hinduism and Islam to look at this theme.

Year 9 How can we answer questions about creation and origins? Learning from religion and science: Christianity, Hinduism, Islam and Atheism. This was an attempt to formalize the presence of other world views apart from the religions in the curriculum.

The syllabus is designed to encourage students to develop a number of skills and understandings. These rest particularly on the ideas of learning about religions (the knowledge base of the subject) and learning from religions (looking at the moral and spiritual questions that the study of religions should encourage students to develop).

Every RE lesson should contain these elements, in the lesson and any written work. The following ideas for the skills and processes are taken from the QCA Scheme of Work and should help to develop your own schemes.

Knowledge, skills and understanding

Learning about religion
1. Pupils should be taught to:
   a. investigate and explain the differing impacts of religious beliefs and teachings on individuals, communities and societies;
   b. analyse and explain how religious beliefs and ideas are transmitted by people, texts and traditions;
   c. investigate and explain why people belong to faith communities and explain the reasons for diversity in religion;
   d. analyse and compare the evidence and arguments used when considering issues of truth in religion and philosophy;
   e. discuss and evaluate how religious beliefs and teachings inform answers to ultimate questions and ethical issues;
   f. apply a wide range of religious and philosophical vocabulary consistently and accurately, recognizing both the power and limitations of language in expressing religious ideas and beliefs;
   g. interpret and evaluate a range of sources, texts and authorities, from a variety of contexts;
   h. interpret a variety of forms of religious and spiritual expression.

Learning from religion
2. Pupils should be taught to:
   a. reflect on the relationship between beliefs, teachings and ultimate questions, communicating their own ideas and using reasoned arguments;
   b. evaluate the challenges and tensions of belonging to a religion and the impact of religion in the contemporary world, expressing their own ideas;
   c. express insights into the significance and value of religion and other world views on human relationships personally, locally and globally;

    d. reflect and evaluate their own and others' beliefs about world issues such as peace and conflict, wealth and poverty and the importance of the environment, communicating their own ideas;

    e. express their own beliefs and ideas, using a variety of forms of expression.

Breadth of study

3. During the key stage, pupils should be taught the Knowledge, skills and understanding through the following areas of study:

Religions and beliefs

a. Christianity.

b. At least two other principal religions.

c. A religious community with a significant local presence, where appropriate.

d. A secular world view, where appropriate..

Themes

a. Beliefs and concepts: the key ideas and questions of meaning in religions and beliefs, including issues related to God, truth, the world, human life, and life after death.

b. Authority: different sources of authority and how they inform believers' lives.

c. Religion and science: issues of truth, explanation, meaning and purpose.

d. Expressions of spirituality: how and why human self-understanding and experiences are expressed in a variety of forms.

e. Ethics and relationships: questions and influences that inform ethical and moral choices, including forgiveness and issues of good and evil.

f. Rights and responsibilities: what religions and beliefs say about human rights and responsibilities, social justice and citizenship.

g. Global issues: what religions and beliefs say about health, wealth, war, animal rights and the environment.

h. Interfaith dialogue: a study of relationships, conflicts and collaboration within and between religions and beliefs.

Experiences and opportunities

a. Encountering people from different religious, cultural and philosophical groups, who can express a range of convictions on religious and ethical issues.

b. Visiting, where possible, places of major religious significance and using opportunities in ICT to enhance pupils' understanding of religion.

c. Discussing, questioning and evaluating important issues in religion and philosophy, including ultimate questions and ethical issues.

d. Reflecting on and carefully evaluating their own beliefs and values and those of others in response to their learning in religious education, using reasoned, balanced arguments.

e. Using a range of forms of expression (such as art and design, music, dance, drama, writing, ICT) to communicate their ideas and responses creatively and thoughtfully exploring the connections between religious education and other subject areas such as the arts, humanities, literature, science.

Differentiation

Since the development of comprehensives and the use of mixed-ability groups for teaching, differentiation has become a key focus of the quality of teaching and learning in a school used by OFSTED. Increasingly, the idea of differentiation by outcome (i.e. that all the class would receive the same tasks and input from the teacher perhaps via a worksheet or a textbook and then pupils would achieve to the levels that they were capable of delivering) has become regarded as unacceptable. Differentiation should be acknowledged in the lesson planning.

There are a number of approaches you could use to foster differentiation in your classroom. Here are some suggestions:

- By the product. You give all the same activity and then measure by the different results or amount of work they produce.
- By the class work/homework set. You give different activities to different pupils who work at different levels. You might also supply different worksheets or other resources in order to help them.
- Input. You might choose to restrict or develop the amount of support given to the pupil by your sense of their ability or level.
- Independent study. You might be responsive to a pupil's desire to study something within a religion and then help them to frame their research topic.

Above all, differentiation means that every pupil should have appropriate and stretching work – in order to make sure that all make progress and that none is left behind.

The language used in many lesson plans does use this. 'All pupils will be able to', 'Most pupils will' and 'Some pupils will' suggest that the teacher should be thinking about developing a set of core skills or knowledge for all students (regardless of ability), some more in-depth knowledge skills/knowledge for the middle/top end of the ability level as well as then helping the gifted and talented end of the class to achieve their potential. The emphasis on personalized learning would seem to suggest that we should go even further and try to think about every individual student.

Following the work of Howard Gardner, the picture of differentiation has become even more complicated. Rather than just thinking in terms of top/middle/lower-level learners, his theories about multiple intelligences have suggested that we see that each person has different skills, different intelligences that need to be catered for. These have often been summarized as visual, audio and kinaesthetic learners. Visual learners like to see things, audio learners like to do things and kinaesthetic learners like to move or be active. The realization that each learner has a learning style is important, so that we can hopefully build connections with them, which will enable them to join in.

One of the criticisms often aimed at RE is a lack of challenge in the classroom. There are several possible ways to approach this:

1. Edward De Bono's six-hats approach. Imagine that you have a variety of hats that reflect different approaches to thinking. This could be used in order to develop some group work, with each of the six types of thinking being represented in the discussions that are to be undertaken:

   a white hat – focus on collecting information
   a yellow hat – focus on being as positive as possible
   black hat – try to be as cautious as possible
   green hat – try to be as creative as possible, 'think outside the box'
   red hat – try to make sure that emotions are thought through
   blue hat – try to consider the big picture

2. Mind mapping – Tony Buzan. Using the mind map can encourage students to see the connections between ideas. It enables them to think about the connections that they can make.

3. A variety of combinations. Students should be able to work in a

number of different combinations. They might work as a pair, trying to gather information. They might then work as a four. There might be time for independent working. We should try to avoid sticking to one method of teaching – not all chalk and talk, but interaction with students. As RE teachers, we might need to particularly emphasize the need to show respect and try to engage with the ideas of others.

4. When writing a scheme of work, try to include a question or exercise that you could set the most able students. In Key Stage 3, why not set a question that is from a GCSE paper or structured like the evaluation questions on the paper? For example:

> 'Gandhi's life was spent campaigning against violence, yet he died a violent death. His life was therefore pointless.' What might a follower of Gandhi say? What do you think? Give reasons for your answer, showing that you have thought about it from more than one point of view.

5. Set a variety of tasks. In a lesson on Moses, I said to pupils that there was a priority task that I expected all to achieve – in this case, some questions from a textbook. Then I listed four other tasks:

   - draw and write about in detail one of the plagues
   - create a crossword with ten clues with words from the story of the Exodus
   - write a poem based on the story of the Passover
   - do further questions from the textbook

   I then went to each student and suggested how many extra tasks I thought they should aim to complete, to encourage challenge and to make them realize how I thought they could deal with having to plan and select their work for themselves without my being totally in control of the order or the priority they gave to it.

   You could also challenge students to develop their own suggestions for work. Try to make sure that they are really challenging themselves and not settling for the line of least resistance.

6. Similarly, develop a writing frame, in which you give pupils key beginnings to sentences so that they can then access a textbook in order to begin to develop their own arguments. Here is an example:

JESUS Writing Frame

Jesus' birth was special because ...
The word Messiah means ...
Jesus' work included ...
When Christians talk about the Passion when referring to Jesus' life, they mean ...

> The Resurrection of Jesus is ...
> Christians have many different beliefs about Jesus. The most important of these are: ...

You can also do this as a variant on a theme, perhaps really useful as a plenary:

> Christians believe that Jesus' death showed the ideas of atonement. This is the idea that Jesus' death showed atonement in two ways.

> This is another variant on the idea of a writing frame, which can also be used as a plenary or as a starter, the binary operations, which we looked at in chapter ....

What is the morality of giving pupils different worksheets? Some people are unhappy with this, as they believe that it can be taken to belittle. Yet, if we have a variety of sheets, can this be mitigated? Any choice of sheets means that you will need to be aware of what each student is using: there is a great temptation for some of the more able students to try to get away with the tasks that they perceive to be the easiest work available to avoid the 'challenge' that OFSTED would want them to have. If you do your work on a computer, it is relatively easy to come up with variant sheets.

Can we realistically expect to get every student's learning right, especially if we are in a situation in which we have a restricted amount of time with them and if we have a huge number of them passing through our doors? Personalized learning is a great idea – but we will need to find ways to make sure that we learn to do it in a way that does not overtax us.

It is also key that when we are trying to differentiate, we make sure that we are setting tasks that extend students rather than repeat their learning about something but in a different way. If we do that, students will become resentful and make them believe that the work is of less value than we would like them to understand. Is a picture really necessary to illustrate the story of David when asking the student to tackle more searching questions might actually be more beneficial?

Ideas for the gifted and talented

In the novel *A Short History of Tractors in Ukrainian* by Marina Lewycka (Penguin, 2006), one character's achievements at GCSE are dismissed, as the only A grade that they are able to achieve is in Religious Studies. We need to challenge this assumption that we have a second-rate subject that is easy and one of the ways in which we do this is by endeavouring to cater for the more able students. Gone are the days when RE could be reduced to colouring in or rote learning of a Biblical story.

It is important that we identify those students whom we believe to be gifted (G) and talented (T). But how can we meet their needs?

1. Projects in Key Stage 3. When we are designing them for both home and class work, do we plan enough to help those who are G and T?
2. GCSE – if we are in a school where the Short Course is followed, we could make sure that G and T pupils follow two short courses, which can, in certain combinations, be put together to achieve a full grade.
3. The A2 route. Another possible way of extending and developing student achievement is to put Key Stage 3 pupils in for A2s in either Religious Studies or Philosophy, which can build upon their understandings.
4. Use of themed days. If your school has a gifted and talented day or has a way of teaching G and T pupils, perhaps by a withdrawal series of lessons, then make sure that RE has input into the scheme. You could work with other departments on a special day – for example, what about a food and faith day with Food Technology? (See the section on curriculum weeks/flexidays).
5. Visits. The use of visits to places of worship or museums that might raise significant moral issues like the Holocaust museum in Derbyshire or the Imperial War Museum can also provide opportunities for the development of more able pupils.

Lesson planning

Lesson planning is one of the most difficult things to get right as a student teacher. The first lesson I ever taught was supposed to last 35 minutes. I was so nervous that I had done my input, got pupils to do written work and then tested them in an informal plenary but then I looked up at the clock and there were still 15 minutes left! I tried to fill using a combination of teacher talk and a spurious task that effectively repeats the earlier written task!

Pace is always an issue for students or NQTs. Pace is either too quick or too slow because the lesson-planning process has not been sufficiently thought through. The three-part lesson has become the standard way to think about lesson planning. First, there should be a starter that engages the pupils and sets the context and content of the lesson. This could be a question. For example, in a lesson on war, you might ask pupils to list the reasons they think are good or morally acceptable reasons for war and those they believe are not. You should also share with the class the objectives you have for this lesson, by putting these on the board. These need to be clear and achievable within the time available. (There are examples of starters and plenaries later in the book.)

Second, there is the development section. This will include some input – textbook, video, discussion, for example – that will result in some pupil work, which could be written. It is important that the development section has shown opportunities for both assessment for learning and for differentiation.

Third, there is the plenary, the way of testing whether learning has taken place and the objectives of the lesson have been fulfilled. You can do this through many different techniques (see my other book, *100 Ideas for Teaching Religious Education* (Continuum, 2008), which contains detailed examples).

The lesson plan should also display the learning outcome for the class. The first outcome should be one achievable by all pupils – high, middle or low ability, 'All pupils should be able to . . .'. The second should be achievable by most of the pupils in the class, 'Most pupils will be able to . . .'. The third outcome will be for the most able in the group, 'Some pupils will be able to . . .'. Differentiation has to be seen in lessons and, increasingly, OFSTED are looking for this by input, not by outcome. Do we have enough resources and individualized work for all pupils to benefit and develop in the lesson?

For RE teachers, this is a very great problem. In most situations, classes are seen only once a week and it will take some planning to be able to create or find resources in order to achieve this.

Look at the following lesson plan example and consider what you might add to it or develop into it to make sure that pupils learnt effectively and there are opportunities to develop assessment for learning.

LESSON PLAN Year 8 Rites of passage: Marriage

Class	Date	Period	Teacher	Ability	Roll
8				Mixed	

LEARNING OBJECTIVES	Key words
(1) All pupils will be able to ... explain the Jewish teachings and practices of marriage. They will be able to give their reflections on marriage.	**Marriage**
(2) Most pupils will be able to ... explain the Jewish teachings and practices of marriage. They will be able to give their reflections on marriage and suggest marriage's strengths and weaknesses.	**Commitment** **Covenant**
(3) Some pupils will be able to ... explain the Jewish teachings and practices of marriage. They will be able to give their reflections on marriage's strengths and weaknesses. They will be able to assess how far they might be suitable for marriage. They will also understand the link between belief and behaviour for religious people in marriage.	**Love** **Arranged marriage**

Timings	
	Starter
5 minutes	What are the reasons people might get married? List them, then discuss them and put them into an order of the best to the worst reasons for marriage OR Write an ad for a potential marriage partner
	Development
5 minutes	1. Follow-up discussion to the starter. Why did people make the choices they did? Write up the five best and five worst reasons on the board.
5 minutes	2. Teacher input: Explain that marriage is a rite of passage, signifying the commitment of two people for each other. This may be done through a secular ceremony or through a religious one. Marriage may be love matches (in which the partners decide for themselves) or arranged marriages (in which their parents may advise or help them to find a partner to marry).
10 minutes	3. Video extract of a Jewish wedding. Ask pupils to note down the symbolism of what they can see and hear.

| 20 minutes | 4. Using a textbook or worksheets, pupils should write about a Jewish marriage and the symbolism involved in it. Provide a writing frame for the less able pupils and a suggestion sheet for what to include for the more able. This is a learning-about task – that is, understanding what religious behaviour and beliefs are and how they affect people. |
| 10 minutes | 5. Set this question, 'Marriage is out of date': What might a Jewish person say to this? What do you think? Give reasons for your answer, showing that you have thought about it from more than one point of view. |

Plenary

As a plenary, you could use the question about what vows you would like to see. How far do these connect with the theme of the lesson?

OR

Write up key words to the Jewish wedding ceremony such as Kiddush, but jumble up the definitions for each of the technical terms, then ask pupils to put the right word and right definition to together.

| Differentiation

Use of writing frames | Special Needs (Support)

There is an assistant to help with Tim Norman |

| Literacy

Using the writing frame
Following the suggestions in order to create their own written work | Numeracy |
| ICT
Could use a writing frame on computer | Health & Safety |
| Homework
Find out about another religious tradition's wedding ceremony | Assessment for learning
Ask pupils to read their answers to the question about marriage and then ask them to evaluate the answers. Give out a couple of examples of good, middling and weak examples. |

Resources
Textbook on Judaism, resource sheets on
Jewish weddings, writing frames. The examples
of answers to the questions to help with
assessment for learning

Photocopy the following lesson plan and try and fill it in for a
subject that you have to do, following the example from the
book.

LESSON PLAN

Class	Date	Period	Teacher	Ability	Roll
8				Mixed	

LEARNING OBJECTIVES	Key words
(1) All pupils will be able to …	
(2) Most pupils will be able to …	
(3) Some pupils will be able to …	

Timings	
	Starter
	Development
	Plenary

Differentiation	Special Needs (Support)
Literacy	Numeracy
ICT	Health & Safety
Homework	Assessment for learning
Resources	

What should characterize learning in a good lesson?

This checklist should help you to devise the perfect lesson! These reflections are based on recent experience of OFSTED. They also try to make sure that good practice in RE is followed as well. You might like to ask yourself how well your lessons measure up against the checklist:

1. Learning intentions are displayed, shared with students and differentiated according to the ability of the class. Make sure that your learning intentions reflect the locally agreed syllabus of the area you are working with. Try to develop the learning about and the learning from strands of the agreed syllabus in your lesson.

2. Teachers differentiate with activities planned to match students'

abilities and needs. Try to be aware and plan for the different learning styles students have.

3. Teaching is consistently challenging, with a wide range of activities planned including pair, group and independent work.

4. Student progress is checked in line with the learning intentions and is at least in line with, or exceeds, the expected progress of that student.

5. Students are aware of the standards required and are constantly involved in their own progression through the sharing of success criteria.

6. Students are able to articulate their level/grade, say whether or not they are on course to achieve their potential and what they need to do to improve.

7. Students are guided to assess their work themselves through peer and self-assessment and are able to identify what they need to do to progress further.

8. Students are assessed regularly and accurately to inform planning for progression.

9. Targets are set that are SMART (short-term, manageable, assessable, realistic and timed).

10. Homework is planned carefully, complementing in-class learning, to promote independent and group learning skills.

11. Any unsatisfactory behaviour or disruption to learning is dealt with quickly and managed effectively by the class teacher in the first instance.

12. Encourage students to show respect to other people's ideas and to articulate their own point of view with clarity.

Writing schemes of work

From surviving the lesson, you need to go on to develop how you plan a group of lessons into a coherent and educational successful whole unit or module.

However, I learnt, and gradually I acquired the skills that are necessary to plan a lesson as well as a scheme of lessons. Now, I seldom just think about the individual lesson, but think about a whole group – normally either in half or full-term modules.

To the person new to education, planning a whole series of lessons seems particularly difficult. As you grow in confidence, these will be easier to do. When planning a series of lessons, start by asking a few questions before doing the detailed work. These questions include the following:

- Will the scheme be about one religion or a number?
- How will it fit in with existing schemes of work? Will its inclusion require another scheme to be revised or dropped?
- If you are planning a scheme on a religion, which topics should you include? Which subjects are not essential? How will you ensure a fair representation of the faith you are studying? (Flip through a few textbooks and you will soon get an impression as to what is important, as will looking at the model syllabus from the QCA.) Are there any members of the religion to be studied in the area or even in the school community who could be useful in helping to develop the scheme?
- If you are taking a theme such as rites of passage or a theme like truth, will there be a coherent thread that links the lessons? Should you try to tackle all key religions or do you select ceremonies/ stories/practices/beliefs that best illustrate the aims?
- How will you make sure that there are a variety of starters and plenary activities?
- How will you make sure differentiation is built into your scheme? Will it stretch the most able and will it also have appropriate strategies/materials for the less able?
- What resources will you need – Worksheets? Textbooks? DVDs? Artefacts?
- How will the scheme reflect the differing learning styles of students?
- Can you use existing materials in a new way?
- How are you going to communicate the ideas behind the scheme so that other members of staff feel that they will be at home with the content, even if they have a different teaching style from the person behind the scheme?

Remember, too, that you should build in times to reflect on whether the scheme needs to be revised or developed. Schemes should not be so rigid that if a teacher has an inspired moment of something not initially written into the scheme, it is excluded.

Textbooks

If you are devising a new scheme of work, it is a sensible idea to buy a selection of possible textbooks. You may decide to focus on using particular texts, but having a variety of support literature is a good idea, as this will help you to develop your understanding of a topic. They might also provide a good source of ideas/

information for worksheets or homework ideas, which a core textbook might lack.

Remember, too, not to be a slave to the way the textbook presents questions. Question styles are constantly evolving and what might seem suitable when it was first published might well change. However, a well written textbook should contain information that can be used to answer new types of questions or activities. Flexibility is the key: the text is the servant of the lesson, not the master.

Try to keep up to date by looking at the website of publishers as well as making sure that you are on their mailing list for catalogues.

Getting balance in your Key Stage 3 curriculum

It is very important that a syllabus is balanced between the needs of informing pupils about Christianity and the world religions. There are legal obligations that require all RE courses in Key Stage 3 to reflect Christianity and at least two other religions in depth.

Case study: Why don't we do Christianity?

Colin is taking a class in Sikhism in Year 8 when a pupil complains that all they ever seem to do in RE are religions other than Christianity. He comes from a Christian background and feels that the school does not do enough on Christianity.

How should Colin explain to him about the importance of teaching him about other faiths? Should Colin check with the Head of Department that there is a balance between Christianity and other religions? Most syllabuses suggest Christianity should have the major place and then two other religions should be taught at Key Stage 3. Is this being honoured?

It is important to explain the importance of studying other religions so that we can have a society that is well informed and tolerant of other faiths. The pupil is probably feeling insecure and therefore he may need to be reassured that the reason for studying other faiths is not to undermine his own faith, but to give him knowledge.

We also need to be increasingly aware of other world views that are not necessarily religious.

Teaching Christianity

In the 1940s, an RE teacher's effectiveness would probably be seen in terms of how many people they had brought to faith in Christianity. With relatively high church and Sunday School attendance, the majority of pupils had a good grasp of Biblical ideas and stories, even some rudimentary understanding of church history.

We do not live in such a society. The stories of the Bible and church history are unknown or not really understood every bit as much as the traditions of the Sikhs or Buddhism. Even when they think they know Christianity, they often do not understand as much as they think they do. I taught one GCSE group a combination of Buddhism and Christianity. When their results were published for the exams, they were widely at odds – they had scored terrifically at Buddhism but where at least two grades lower each in Christianity. They had not understood Christianity as much as I had thought and I had failed to take account of the fact that they might need things about Christianity explained more, not less, than Buddhism.

We must begin by assuming that students know less than we think and that even what they appear to know is not always understood. Many students think that Good Friday has to be linked to Jesus' Resurrection, as they are unable to get the symbolic naming of the day.

Look at these contributions from an email that a friend once passed to me. They are all howlers that were found in tests and exams:

> When Mary heard she was the mother of Jesus, she sang the Magna Carta.
> When the Three Wise Guys from the East Side arrived they found Jesus in the Manager.
> The people who followed the Lord were called the 12 decibels.
> The Epistels were the wives of the apostles.

These do exaggerate the situation, yet they also contain a truth: we live in a post-Christian society, in which many think they know things, yet do not. We should try to make sure that all students have an understanding of Christianity, as not to have this will mean that they are not fully aware of the roots and development of culture, arts and morality, let alone religion and its influence in our public life.

We need to find ways that present the life of Jesus in a new, imaginative way. One way to start could be to look at the paintings and iconography associated with Christ. Then you should inform students of the fact that nowhere in the Gospels or any other ancient writings is there any description of what Jesus looked like. This gives us a good basis of discussion – why should this be of no importance to the disciples?

Another way to engage students is to get them involved in the debate about miracles, especially with regards to those claimed to be Jesus'. One way of treating the Resurrection stories is as a detective story, as Chris Wright does in his book on Christianity for Lion in the 1980s.

We should explore the parables as well. Think about the emotions that might go through the three principal characters in the story of the Prodigal Son in Luke 15. How might charting their emotions influence the way you could re-tell the story? What can you learn about the story if you were to re-tell it from the point of view of each of the three main characters – the elder son, the Father and the younger son? One group of pupils once challenged one RE teacher as to where the mother was in this story and whether her absence made this story happen.

We also need to explore the drama of the Passion Week. There are some role-plays that don't require much preparation, which might help students to understand the importance of Holy Week. How about this one to illustrate Palm Sunday? Ask one student to leave the room. Brief the class to stand up and clap when the person comes back in. Then, after the student has sat down, ask another student to go outside and then come back in. This time, the class have to boo and give them a slow handclap. This will hint at the different reactions Jesus got in Holy Week – from popularity to rejection.

You might like to encourage students to make their own Resurrection garden. Take a tray and put some earth in it. Using pebbles and other materials, make a tomb as well as the angels and the women who were there.

You might like to encourage pupils to develop a story board

about a key story, such as the Road to Emmaus story in Luke 24.

Teaching the Bible

The work of Loukes and Goldman in the 1960s aimed to prove that the way the Bible was taught in schools was not appropriate. They were right, but, as a consequence, too many schools began to lose confidence in teaching the Bible at all. Yet, in order for a pupil to achieve their entitlement to understand the culture and the practices of the United Kingdom, an understanding of the Bible and its place in shaping things is essential.

James Barr once described the Bible as 'a bomb of a book' – a phrase that suggests that it is radical, disturbing in its content and its message. Too much RE has really gone out of its way to reduce the Bible to a bomb with no fuse, a damp firework that seemingly can never be re-lit.

To teach the Bible effectively, we need to think of the process as dealing with code. Take the story of Cain and Abel. What has that to say to modern society? The themes of jealousy, siblings, judgement, murder and personal accountability are all there. That story can become, even for pupils who are not religious, a way to help them.

You can also examine the idea of prophecy – how the Biblical prophets speak for God about what is wrong with society and calling them in the name of God to repent. Then, they also give the people a vision of the better world. One way to show the relevance of this would be to look at the way in which Martin Luther King uses the prophetic language in speeches like 'I Have a Dream'.

A few years ago, I asked pupils to write about the relevance of the Bible to life. Many could not make connections with their lives or anyone else's. One male did. He began by telling how he was not religious but how he had found the story of David and Goliath helpful in that he saw himself as David, confronted by a whole set of personal and family crises that seemed to be towering over him like the Philistine giant. The story gave him hope that the small or the powerless can triumph, however the circumstances might seem. He had learnt to use the Bible in a metaphorical sense to help him. He knew about the power of story to transform and inform what he was going through.

We might need to use a variety of approaches. Think for a moment how the following might help you:

- Liberation theology, centred on God's concern for the poor.
- Feminist theology – trying to see things from a feminist point of view.
- Typology – what types or archetypes do we see in the stories?
- Narrative theology – how is the story formed and why is it important to the community of faith?

It is important for students to see that there is a diversity of ways of interpreting the Bible. They need to realize that some see the Bible as standing unerring forever whilst others see the Bible as containing ideas that are applied or discarded as they fit with the world around us. It is very important that students see that not all Christians have a 'fundamentalist' view of Scripture but they realize that the debate about the Bible is still ongoing.

Teaching creeds

If you are to teach Christianity, then you need at some point to give time to teaching creeds. Yet, how are we to make the language of faith that these contain immediate and of relevance to pupils who may not understand what they are reading?

We need to begin by challenging them to realize that they are believers – in something.

We need to get them to think about the different types of belief – in a historical fact like the Norman invasion of 1066, in their football team, in the love or not of their parents, in their favourite music or in the social values that they may have, like being against racism and sexism. How far can they prove these beliefs? Which really motivate and change their behaviour? Which are beliefs that have no consequence?

You could encourage pupils to develop their own creedal statements. You might like to see if you could get the entire class to see whether they can come up with a creed for the class that reflects all the views of its members.

Look at the Apostles' Creed below. How might you explain some of the key terms here? One way to help students to unpack this might be to get them to do some type of mime or movement – so what might work with these words?

I believe in God, the Father Almighty, the Creator of heaven and earth, and in Jesus Christ, His only Son, our Lord: Who was conceived of the Holy Spirit, born of the Virgin Mary, suffered under Pontius Pilate, was crucified, died, and was buried.

He descended into hell.

The third day He arose again from the dead.

He ascended into heaven and sits at the right hand of God the Father Almighty, whence He shall come to judge the living and the dead.

I believe in the Holy Spirit, the holy catholic church, the communion of saints, the forgiveness of sins, the resurrection of the body, and life everlasting.

Amen.

Another approach might be to give them a copy of the Creed and to underline every word or phrase that they do not understand.

Alternatively, you could cut the Creed into strips and then ask them to re-construct it into an order that seems to be coherent, then justify their choices to the class.

Language for learning about Christianity

RE is one of the subjects that need to place a great emphasis on the idea of students' learning words that are key to explain the subject. The model syllabuses that the faith communities and educational experts came together to write in the 1990s have become the standard for both the spelling and the meaning of terms used. These are available from the QCA and have been used to inform the work of SACREs and the exam boards when drawing up their syllabuses.

It is a good idea to supply students with a list of key words, especially when they are preparing for GCSE. You might also like them to develop their own dictionary of relevant terms. One of the biggest obstacles to achieving the higher levels in Key Stage 3 and the best GCSE grades in Key Stage 4 is the fact that many students do not have a sufficiently wide or accurate vocabulary in order to help them to frame their ideas into the sophisticated arguments that are needed to achieve all that they can. Students should have the key terms and meanings of words from Christianity. Look at the following list:

Adoration	Heaven	Pharisee
Anglican	Hell	Protestant
Ascension	Intercession	Purgatory
Baptism	Jesus	Resurrection
Christ	Limbo	Roman Catholic
Communion	Lord's Supper	Sadducee
Confession	Mass	Second Coming
Crucifixion	Messiah	Speaking in tongues
Disciple	Miracle	Temptation
Epistle	Nativity	Testament
Eucharist	Orthodox	
Gospel	Parable	

Artefacts for teaching Christianity

A well run RE department should try to develop a collection of artefacts. It is important when you buy artefacts that you try to avoid the most lurid or inappropriate. The impression given by the use of the right artefact can be profound, but so can the use of a less than impressive one.

Following is a list of the artefacts from Christianity that would be very useful to have in order to help students to understand Christianity:

Icons	Chalice
Crucifixes	Statue of the Virgin Mary
Palm cross	Festal candles
Bible	Selection of Christmas cards –
Bible reading notes	religious and non-religious
Prayer books	Salvation Army flag
Rosary	Postcards of the Holy Land
Fish badge	Postcards of the Vatican
Advent calendar	Images from the Turin Shroud
Dove symbol	CDs of traditional and contemporary
Baptismal shell	worship music
Crib with figures	

The use of images could be very informative. Take a selection of the images you might get on Christmas cards – what do they reveal about beliefs about Jesus and Mary? Another question to look at is why, if the Easter festival is so important, are there many fewer Easter cards sent than Christmas ones?

A study of icons and their history can also be very good at making pupils thinking about the importance of imagery of the divine. Perhaps you could get students to make their own stained-glass images by using black paper and see-through coloured paper.

Teaching other world religions

'Are you a Buddhist, Mr Wood?' This is a question that I have been asked frequently by pupils when teaching that religion. I am not, but if that question is asked, I am pleased. When I first started teaching, Buddhism was the religion that I knew least about, so I set about reading everything I could and talking to Buddhists. Eventually, I even ended up writing a textbook on it – not bad for an Evangelical Christian!

It seems to me that the job of the RE teacher should be to act as a defence lawyer for a client – I may not completely relate to the client (religion) but I have learnt to put their ideas and practices in way that is understandable and does not reinforce prejudice or stereotypes.

The RE teacher must make sure that they are familiar with what terms mean. Try to avoid the temptation to read a word quickly from the textbook when you are not really sure what it means, in the hope that somehow you will get away with not being challenged by the pupils you teach to explain their meaning and context! They will spot this and, if you fluff it, be honest. Try to talk to a member of the faith that you are studying and ask them to tell you how to pronounce any difficult words.

Accuracy is important in teaching world faiths. Recently, we decided that we needed to improve the Islam course that we were teaching. We decided that, as well as investing in new textbooks, we should ask Muslim pupils to tell us what they thought about the existing course and help us to prioritize what the most important things we should teach about Islam would be.

The courses we devise must accurately reflect the beliefs and practices of adherents, seeking not to put a spin or a gloss on what they believe, but to give an accurate representation. We will need to keep having such conversations with students in order to help to update and develop our knowledge.

It is important that, when teaching other religions, access to meeting members of those faiths or being able to visit the places of worship is made a priority. All the textbooks in the world are not as effective as meeting or seeing a worshipping community in action.

Teaching Judaism

Any course on Judaism should contain material from the Bible, an explanation of key ceremonies, moral/religious understanding as well as the development of Judaism. The history of the Jews is also a high priority, as theology and history are interwoven in their sense of identity.

Following is a list of key words and phrases that need to be included in any course on Judaism.

Language for learning about Judaism

Ark	Ner Tamid
Bar Mitzvah	Oral Law
Bat Mitzvah	Orthodox Jews
Bimah	Passover
Cantor	Patriarch
Challah	Pentecost
Circumcision	Pesach
Covenant	Purim
Diaspora	Rabbi
Exodus	Shabbat
Gregger	Shalom
Hanuakkah	Shema
Huppah	Shiva
Kaddish	Sukkot
Ketubah	Synagogue
Kippah	Tallit
Kosher	Talmund
Menorah	Tefillin
Mezuzah	Torah
Minyan	Yad
Mishnah	Yom Kippur
Mohel	Zionism
Monotheism	

Artefacts for teaching Judaism

To help you to teach Judaism, the following would be very useful for you to own, so that reconstructions of festivals can be made possible, for example:

Menorah	Sabbath candlesticks
Kippah (skull cap)	Tallith
Seder plate	Teffillin
Matzos box	Yad
Kiddush cup	Scrolls (mini, with scroll cover like
Challah loaf	the scrolls in the synagogue)
Havadalah set	Shofar horn
Mezuzah	Drediel

These artefacts may help you to stage re-constructions of the key festivals, such as the Passover and Purim, which will enable students to understand by action as well as reading about the faith.

By looking at Jewish rites of passage, such as Bar and Bat Mitzvah, you will help students to reflect on what is meant by the concept of maturity. Examinations of Jewish marriage and funerals can also encourage them to think through their ideas about commitment and how to mourn the death of someone they love.

A trip to a synagogue will enable students to see the power of symbolism and worship within Judaism. It will also give them the opportunity to ask questions of the members of the faith in person rather than second hand, as they do when they ask most RE teachers.

With the teaching of Judaism, there is always an elephant in the room that cannot ever be avoided: the Holocaust. How we teach this needs careful thought.

Teaching the Holocaust

In Alan Bennett's play, *The History Boys* (DVD, 2007), there is a very powerful scene in which two teachers taking a group of boys studying for entrance exams into Oxford or Cambridge University begin to debate the Holocaust. Can you look at it objectively? The play is set in 1983 and one character concludes that you cannot do so, as it is the recent past.

Time has moved on. When I first began teaching, it was

difficult to imagine a holocaust happening again in Europe. Then came Bosnia, Kosovo. We realized, too, that holocausts happen in places like Cambodia or Rwanda or Darfur in the Sudan.

How should we teach about the Holocaust? Should it just be contained within a module about Judaism? We need to tell this story as part of Judaism, but we also need to tell it as a story about humanity's evil and, in some cases, greatness in the face of suffering.

There is a danger that we can distort the event – what of those of other religions such as Christians who died? The Holocaust was also racial, homophobic and directed at those with learning or physical disabilities. Should we tell their stories?

Just to remind you how this issue is alive, look at the following case study.

Case study: If I ruled the world

Kathy set her class an exercise that was called 'If I ruled the world', hoping to use this as the basis of a discussion about the idea of God being in control. One child, called Michael, wrote, 'If I ruled the world, I would not want there to be any blacks or Jews'.

Kathy asked Michael to read this aloud and could not conceal her shock at what he had written. Some members of the class were shocked. Kathy tried not to look too angry, thinking that probably what Michael wrote may well have been what his parents said. She said gently, 'That wasn't really appropriate'.

At the end of the lesson, she talked to Michael, who did say that what he had written had been a result of things he had overheard at home. But what should she do now?

There is no easy solution to this. Kathy acted wisely in trying to defuse the situation and by talking to the child at the end of the lesson in order to make sure that he was aware of what she regarded as acceptable and quite possibly what the school anti-racist policy was. She tried not to undermine what the child's parents had said but to talk about the appropriateness of what was said in the task. As teachers of RE, we must be seen to be fair but firm about this issue. The child also needs to be made aware of the Holocaust and slavery, to help them realize that suffering and injustice is no way to a perfect world.

The Holocaust, though, is not primarily an opportunity to reflect on an historical event for the RE teacher – it raises vital spiritual and moral questions. In William Stryon's novel, *Sophie's Choice* (Corgi, 1983), two questions are raised by a central character about what has happened:

Where was God?
Where was Man?

Both God and humanity have questions to face about the suffering that people experienced. Whilst a good RE lesson will enable pupils to see the historical context of events like the Holocaust, it is failing to be RE if it does not provoke questions like those that Stryon's character posed. Any module on Judaism has to have some reference to the Holocaust, be that an examination of the story of Anne Frank or a look at the writings of Elie Wiesel, both of whom were of secondary-school age when they experienced the anti-Semitism and concentration camps' genocide.

The ideas of evil and suffering in the Holocaust will inevitably be opened up but so should questions about justice, the unselfishness of many camp survivors and the consequences for the world around us.

The non-statutory schemes have, as we have seen, encouraged us to examine what happened to the Jews after these events, as one section covers another problem – the ownership of religious sites in Jerusalem.

Case study: Parent's complaint about teaching the Holocaust

Penny has been teaching her class about the Holocaust. In order to help pupils to understand this, she photocopied a series of photographs and other images from the time. She stuck them up around her classroom. She invited pupils to wander round and look at these images, to take their time and consider what the images mean.

One of her pupils, Jessica, went home and, when asleep, had a nightmare about the Holocaust. Her mother wrote to the school, suggesting that when they teach about the issue, they should not use images that might disturb pupils.

What should Penny do? Was she wrong to use the images she did? How might her Head of Department help her? Should the RE department write to Jessica's mother?

Using images to teach the Holocaust seems to be inevitable as a teaching technique and it is also a very powerful way of engaging students' understanding of the subject matter. If the only reason for the selection is to shock, then this may mean that it is not necessarily meeting its educational aims, so care should be taken on this. Indeed, Penny's approach is a powerful and involving one: it is what the visitor experiences when going to the Yad Vashem Holocaust Museum in Jerusalem or even the Imperial War Museum in London.

Penny needs to talk through the issues raised by the letter with the Head of Department and then work out whether she or the Head of Department should respond to the letter. It cannot go unchallenged.

The Holocaust may shock and disturb, but we need to be true to the events and make sure that students are educated to deal with their emotions every bit as much as the historical realities of the events. Not to educate in an appropriate way will be to deny students a proper education.

Teaching Islam

Since the rise of political Islam in Iran in the 1970s, teaching Islam has become ever more difficult. Since the events of 9/11, it has become even more necessary in order to counter Islamaphobia and help in developing understanding. How we deal with the issue will be crucial as to how far our students can deal with the nature of Islam, understanding that extremism is a minority issue.

Case study: The offensive teddy bear

In December 2007, English primary school teacher Gillian Gibbons was put in prison in Sudan for allowing a class to name a teddy bear Muhammad. She went to prison for over a week and, following the intervention of politicians from the UK, she was released.

Ben is a new teacher in a school and has a Year 7 module to teach on Islam. How should he respond if he were asked about a case like the Gillian Gibbons one? Should he change the subject or should he try to address the issue head on? How should he tackle it if there are Muslim pupils in the class?

How would you deal with this? Is a quick answer going to help or hinder understanding? Caution is important. You may need to think through the consequences of any answer you give, especially if there are members of the faith involved in the room. You don't have to answer, and it might not be wise to, until all the facts are known and perhaps a little time has passed to take the heat out of the problem.

We also need to show that this story had a variety of responses from Muslims. We need to question the images of Muslims and Islam in the media, to encourage students to be critical of the messages they receive.

Language for learning about Islam

These words and phrases should be taught as part of a module on Islam, so that students are given a full understanding of the faith:

Adhan	Mihrab
Akhirah	Minaret
Allah	Minbar
Du'a	Mosque
Hadiths	Pbuh
Hajii	Prophets
Hajj	Qu'ran
Halal	Ramadan
Hijab	Rislah
Id-Adha	Salah
Id-ul-Fitr	Sawm
Ihram	Shahadah
Imam	Shaytan
Islam	Shirk
Jihad	Surah
Kabbah	Tawhid
Khalifah	Ummah
Khitan	Wudu
Madrasha	Zakah

Check that you know the precise meaning of each of the words or phrases on the list.

Artefacts for teaching Islam

You will also benefit from having some artefacts for the teaching of Islam. These could include the following:

The Qu'ran
Qu'ran stand
Compass to find Makkah
Prayer mat
Large postcard of the Kaaba
Examples of Islamic calligraphy
Prayer beads
Model of a mosque
Map of Islamic countries in the world

Teaching Hinduism

Teaching Hinduism will require thoughtful preparation, as it is easy to present the faith in a somewhat crass way. You will need to talk about the ideas of God, such as the Trimurti, the use of images, the importance of worship, the caste system and the rites of passage.

You ought to make sure that students know how Hindus have been influenced by thinkers and activists like Gandhi, as well as reflect on the experience of Hindu communities in the UK.

Language for learning about Hinduism

These words and phrases should be taught as part of a module on Hinduism:

Ahimsa	Japii
Ashram	Mandir
Atman	Satya
Avatar	Shiva
Brahma	Swastikia
Brahman	Untouchable
Brahmin	Varna
Caste	Vishnu

Artefacts for teaching Hindu

The following artefacts will be worth having when you are teaching Hinduism:

Murtis, such as of Ganesh, Krishna, Shiva, Hanuman
Devas
Joss sticks

OM sign
Swastika
Mendhi kit
Divali card
Krishna's flute
Prayer shawl
Model of a mandir, the Hindu temple

A visit to Hindu temples will also help students to think about the role of religion in the believers' lives: I have included the addresses of a couple of well known mandir in the resources section of the book.

Teaching Buddhism

Buddhism can be taught in a number of exciting ways. Looking at the birth story of the Buddha is important to help students to think about the way myth and legend contribute to religious understanding as well as history.

Discussions about the importance of beliefs like the Four Noble Truths or the moral teachings of the Five Moral Precepts can be stimulating, as can a look at the alternative community of the Buddhist convent or monastery. You can encourage pupils into an active learning strategy by trying meditation with a group. An appreciation of the art of Buddhism such as the madala is important. The fashionable use of Buddhist images of the Buddha ('isn't he a fat bloke?') needs to be examined and students given insight into its importance to believers.

Language for learning about Buddhism

The following words or phrases are essential for students to know when studying Buddhism:

Ananda	Eightfold Path
Asceticism	Enlightenment
Bhikku	Five moral precepts
Bodh Gaya	Four Noble Truths
Bodhisattva	Karma
Braham Viharas	Karuna
Buddha	Kisagami
Dalai Lama	Kusingara
Dharma	Lumbini Grove

Mahaynna Buddhism
Mala Beads
Mandalas
Mara
Meditation
Metta
Middle Way
Nibbana/Nirvana
Pali Canon
Pitaka
Rahula
Sangha

Sarnath
Siddharta Gautama
Songkran
Stupa
Theravada Buddhism
Three Refugees
Tripitaka
Wat
Wesak
Wheel of Life
Yashodhara

Artefacts for teaching Buddhism

These might prove to be very useful to you when you are teaching Buddhism:

Buddha statues
Selection of postcards of the Buddha
Mala beads
Wheel of Life poster
Alms bowl
Butter lamp for Wesak
Prayer wheel
Chou Gong

Visits to Buddhist viharas or monasteries will also help students to understand the faith more.

Teaching Sikhism

The youngest of the six largest world faiths, Sikhism has been shaped by its interactions with both Hinduism and Islam as well as developing its own distinctive approaches to the issues of the world. The existence of large Sikh communities in areas like Southall, Leicester and Bradford is a fascinating study of immigrant life and how communities reinvent themselves, whilst trying to retain their culture. (The film *Bend It Like Beckham* (DVD, 2002) brilliantly and comically explores some of these issues.)

Language for learning about Sikhism

These words and phrases should be in any module about Sikhism:

Adi Granth	Karah Prashad
Amrit	Karma
Amritsar	Kaur
Ardas	kesh
Baisakhi	Khalsa
Caste	Khanda
Chanani	Kirpan
Chauri	Kirtan
Divali	Langar
Diwan	Lavan
Five KS	Mela
Golak	Mool Mantar
Granthi	Nishan Sahib
Gurdwara	Panj Kakke
Gurpurbs	Romalla
Guru	Sadsangat
Guru Gobind Singh	Sewa
Guru Nanak	Sikh
Gurumurki	Singh
Ik Onkar	Turban
Kangha	Waheguru
Kara	

Artefacts for teaching Sikhism

The following might help in the teaching of Sikhism:

The five Ks – the comb (kanga), the hair (kesh – represented by a turban), the dagger (kirpan), the underpants (kacheara) and the bangle (kara)

Nishan Sahib flag

Pictures of the Ten Gurus, especially Guru Nanak and Guru Gobind Singh

Statue of Guru Nanak

Karah Parshad bowl

Ik onkar symbol

Sari

Postcards of the Golden Temple and other Gurdwaras

A general note on artefacts – how might you use them in a classroom? Artefacts are important, as they symbolically contain many messages about the religion. Take the Seder plate of Judaism. This shows the story of the Passover but it also talks about Elijah, hopes for Jews to go to Jerusalem and Old Testament history. Yet, it will also have a powerful new context, as Jews reflect on the 'slavery' their people faced in the concentration camps in the Second World War. Artefacts therefore both retain and can develop meeting. After all, the bread at the Passover and the wine at the Passover were appropriated by Jesus to help form the Last Supper. It is important to let students realize that some artefacts have a similar story, but can be used in different ways.

Artefacts can be used to draw or to be re-created. You might like to ask a student what the message behind the object is and then try to re-express that in another physical shape.

For many pupils, touching or using their other senses on the artefact is an important way to learn what is truly important, as that will enable them to develop a good memory of the artefact's meaning and purpose, rather than just seeing a photograph in a book or its being described. It is also important to encourage them to explore the idea of reverence and respect in the way they might hold or pass on the artefact to another person.

Try to display artefacts in your classroom. A colleague of mine always has one on her desk each week, in order to provoke discussion with students who enter her room and therefore help develop their learning.

Encouraging pupils to make their own artefacts or to reflect on what they own that is of supreme importance to them means a great deal to them.

Other world views

'I don't have any beliefs,' many pupils might say. Really? Probably what they mean is that they do not have any religious beliefs. Here, again, things might not be as they seem, as they might actually have beliefs that are religious but they may not be aware of their original context (e.g. a belief in reincarnation or some type of life after death might fit this). Their beliefs about anti-sexism, anti-racism, the importance of their music taste and what rights they are entitled to, give the lie to the idea that they are belief-less. They are belief-full and need to learn to see themselves as people with commitments and values.

We live in an increasingly complex world, in which both religious and non-religious ideas are part of the society our pupils live in. The works of Richard Dawkins and Christopher Hitchens may not be widely read by pupils, but the popular versions of what they say are very likely to influence their worlds.

'Religion has been disproved by science' is a phrase that you might often hear, but how are you going to respond to this somewhat simplistic slogan? Or how about this one: 'If God really exists, why is there suffering in this world?'

Since the Birmingham Agreed Syllabus of 1975 encouraged the examination of Humanism and Communism as world views, there has been a growing tendency to examine the atheist, agnostic or materialist secularist responses to faith. These need to be explored as options in some way.

We also need to realize the post-modern mindset that many students have, who are comfortable to mix and match a number of beliefs that in the past may not have been seen to logically cohere. Students may increasingly get their views from the media – a satellite TV programme about ghost hunting might seem to have as much rationality to some students as science and/or religion. Explorations or questioning of realities in films like *The Matrix* or the excitement of a grand myth such as you find in *Harry Potter*, *Narnia* and the *Lord of the Rings* show that there are possible spiritual points of connection.

Certainly, many students have often a pragmatic, relative view of morality rather than a sense of absolutism, which is key to remember when we might try to start a lesson by suggesting that there is a moral debate. We need to encourage them to see the alternatives.

Pedagogy in RE

Teaching in themes

Traditionally, RE has been driven by a desire to (a) look in depth at a world religion, (b) study a particular cross-religious theme like pilgrimage or worship, (c) concentrate on a religious person, be that Jesus, Muhammad or more recent figures like Gandhi or Martin Luther King, and (d) investigate a moral issue such as war, abortion or poverty.

Syllabuses in RE are not always constructed around the discrete teaching of world religions. Teaching cross-religious modules has been popular. Some of these could include:

Founders of religion
Creation stories
Beliefs about life after death
Rites of passage
Science and religion
Teaching on poverty/the environment/racism

These can be very rewarding, but unless you are very careful, they can lead to confusion, with students not understanding the context of a religion or blurring the distinctiveness of religion. Get it right and they can see the things that religions may well hold in common. Get it wrong and they will see all religions as the same and not be able to think about their distinctiveness.

Following is another suggestion that might fit with a school programme to help to develop more than just the academic side of a student.

Emotional intelligence

Increasingly, education is drawing upon the ideas of emotional intelligence in order to develop students. Should not our curriculum choices reflect that we all work in emotional contexts that affect our performance?

Why don't we shift to thinking about the possibility of a curriculum – at least in part – that addresses the emotional development of students? This does not have to be the province of PSHE or Tutorial time, but can be the focus of personal and emotional development.

Think about these themes that could be used to experiment with an emotionally intelligent RE:

1. Anger – is it wrong? Can it be appropriate? You could use the story of Cain and Abel as an example of inappropriate anger (caused by jealousy) in contrast to Jesus' action against the traders in the Temple (anger at injustice and corruption). Other examples would include Muhammad's anger at the corruption in Makkah.
2. Love. The different types of love. The ideas of love in 1 Corinthians 13. Forgiveness as shown on the Cross. The love of the members of the Khalsa in Sikhism or the Ummah in Islam.
3. Fear for the future/worry. How religious ideas might deal with this: the prophetic hopes of the Old Testament or the visions of Revelation. Jesus' teaching on worry.
4. Selfishness. The teaching of Jesus and the Buddha on selfishness. How might that challenge students to think about the way in which they live?

What other emotions might you like to address?

Philosophy

It has become very popular to use ideas from philosophy to help in RE. Philosophy is about asking the right questions, clarifying terms and trying to see whether there can be answers (however) provisionally to life.

You could use the strategy known as the community of enquiry, in which you ask students to work on a set of questions together. One classic way of doing this is to give students a scenario like this. Imagine they are cast away with a small community of other people on a desert island. What rules might they need to have in order to make sure that the community functions effectively? What might they need to do?

Using philosophy can be difficult unless the teacher has a fair grasp. Books like *Sophie's World* (Berkley, 1996) by Josteen Garnier or Alain De Botton's *The Consolations of Philosophy* (Penguin, 2004) are excellent at digesting difficult ideas and putting them across in a way that is accessible to those not aware of them.

Helping students to see that religions are often asking fundamental questions that all people ask – religious or not – is really important. The questions about reality – what is real and what isn't – are vital to postmodernism and are reflected in much of TV and cinema that students see.

A recent RE publication made a link between the story of Plato's cave (in which people trapped in a cave are unsure whether the images they see reflected in the cave are real or shadow, so question the whole notion of being) and the film *The Matrix*. Both of them deal with the issues of what is real and what is imagined. This is increasingly a problem that students are interested in. Other questions that they will be interested in include:

> How do we know what is true?
> Where do we get a sense of right and wrong?
> What is evil?
> Why is there suffering?
> Is there a god?
> Is this life all there is – or is there a life after death?

It is important that we have materials to use in class that reflect both religious and non-religious answers to these questions and that we allow those students who can never accept a religious conclusion space in order to express their views. It is important that students should be encouraged to see that some of these questions may be unanswerable.

Using role-play

The most important issue with role-play is preparation. If you are not properly prepared, then it can be the worst of experiences; if you are prepared, then it can be one of the best!

One way to structure role-play is to put students into groups of three – one to present a role-play, one to act as the scribe for the ideas and another to help with ideas. This will enable those students are who are shy or might find themselves tongue-tied to still contribute to the lesson, but without feeling threatened.

Role-plays are especially good for bringing out issues with regards to morality such as abortion or war. It is important that you give students a precise description of a character to assume in a role-play. For example, in a role-play about war, you might have the following characters:

> General Tom – an army commander. He believes in the Just War theory. As a believing Christian, he believes that he has the responsibility to care for the weak or powerless.
>
> Karen Peace – a pacifist. She believes that Christ has forbidden Christians from fighting, as he said that they should not strike back, that they should love their enemies and that 'those who live by the sword will die by the sword'.

In order to do this role-play, you would need to make sure that the first group has the Just War theory whilst the second would need extracts from the Sermon on the Mount. As the teacher, you will need to help students make the connections between the beliefs and the characters, which is a vital skill. Students need to make the connection between beliefs and behaviour, which is a key skill, especially at GCSE level. This also makes the connection between learning about and learning from religion, which underlies agreed syllabuses.

Another way you could run a role-play is to use the device of a television discussion programme. Appoint a panel and a chair. They will research a topic, with the panel writing speeches and the chair writing some questions with which he can challenge the panel members. Have a set of questions prepared that you can give to the remaining members of the class, so that they can all take part or, if you are feeling confident, ask them to generate their own. Try not to let it descend into abuse – either personal or about people's ideas. Encourage students to show respect to others, whatever their feelings about their views might be.

Make sure that when you are running a role-play, you:

1. Give enough time for planning the speech/contribution by the character. It is probably best to have a lesson to prepare and then a lesson to present/run.
2. When the role-play is running, the characters are not interrupted whilst giving their contribution.
3. You have enough time to allow for cross-questioning. Try to get as

many people involved as possible. For the shyer or less confident, why not ask the class to write down questions anonymously and then be the spokesperson for the group?

Make sure that you have clear objectives – what, for example, do you want the class to know about the morality of war or abortion?

Not all classes are capable of running a role-play, for all kinds of reasons – so, if you have not done so before, start with the group that you have fewest problems with and are the most positive about the subject. This will help you to develop your confidence with this technique.

You might also like to run a more conventional 'This house believes' type of debate, with a proposer and an opposer.

Citizenship in Religious Education

Citizenship became a compulsory subject in 2002. It also is increasingly influencing the teaching of all subjects in the curriculum, with OFSTED keen to find Citizenship themes addressed in other subject areas. RE gives many different opportunities to help develop Citizenship. Citizenship may well have a similarity of content (e.g. social and religious diversity), skills and is about developing attitudes such as understanding and tolerance.

As excellent RE focuses on how the topics are relevant to the life of the student (the learning-from strand), Citizenship themes will often be addressed. A lesson on Abraham with Years could look at whether Abraham was a hero or a villain, if he was a model citizen or not. Religious and non-religious theories about war as well as studying the lives of Gandhi, Martin Luther King or Mother Teresa or the debate about the Hijab all have the capability to be issues that can develop Citizenship.

The QCA provide an exemplar of how RE and Citizenship education can work in harmony at www.standards.dfes.gov.uk.

It is a good idea to regularly audit your curriculum to make sure that Citizenship is being covered. If your department has not already got a copy, get hold of *Making Sense of Citizenship: A Continuing Professional Development Handbook*, edited by Ted Huddleston and David Kerr (Hodder Murray/The Citizenship Foundation, 2006).

If your school has themed days or weeks in order to teach

students Citizenship skills, make sure that your department plays an active role – for example, anti-racism week could include material from the Holocaust or the struggles of Christians against racism across the world. Many schools also have tutorial and assembly programmes that reflect Citizenship themes: would it be a good idea to offer to do an assembly that shows the link between RE and Citizenship? However, make sure that your assembly is as good as it can be, as one bad assembly can undermine a great deal of good work in the classroom!

Citizenship also provides another impetus to talking to local religious and campaigning groups, so that they might develop links with your school and your subject. Visiting religious buildings and local museums can also help to develop good citizenship, as can organizing a charity fund-raising event with the local community.

Starters and plenaries

There are a variety of different approaches that you can take in order to introduce or consolidate learning. Here is a selection. (You will find other suggestions in my *100 Ideas for Teaching Religious Education*, Continuum, 2008.)

Spider diagrams/mind maps

Take a topic and the question at the heart of it and then ask students to explore it by producing their own responses. For example, as an introduction to a lesson on the importance of Gurus in Sikhism, write the question 'What makes a good teacher?' in the centre of the board, asking them to write down as many qualities individually as they can.

After 2 minutes, ask them to swap their lists and try to add to these. Then call all the class together to try to come up with the best list possible.

Another way of doing this is just to put the topic up, such as the environment or Islam, to see what words or phrases students connect with the topic. This will help you to see the areas that you might need to address, especially if it reveals popular prejudices or misconceptions.

Card sort

Have a series of cards with the key issues or ideas that you wish to explore in a lesson. Take a theme like miracles. Write a selection of different opinions on cards and then ask students to sort these. If you can, make a board with a diamond nine into which they must then put them in order of importance or possible acceptability to the group.

Photographs

Give groups in a class a photograph and ask them to comment on what they see. You could cover up or remove a vital section, to help them question the assumptions of students. For example, when you are doing a subject like poverty or war, give the group an image that might question or provoke their ideas about the topic.

The Venn diagram

The Venn diagram from mathematics can be useful in RE. By asking students to put information in either one circle or another or write it in the middle, you will be able to help them to process information on a topic, overlaps and the differences between religions or stories. The Venn diagram enables pupils to see these clearly. They then can begin to see areas on which they disagree and where they coincide. This could also help weaker pupils to develop their extended writing.

Discussion starters

Another approach – particularly if you think that your class might get out of hand if given a group of cards – is to give them an A4 sheet with different ideas, from which they then have to choose three and write a couple of sentences about each. For example, you might offer the following discussion starter sentences on war:

> *War is hell*
> *War – what is it good for? Absolutely nothing!*

War is a necessary evil
There are wars that have to be fought for there to be justice
The use of a nuclear weapon can never be justified

You must make sure that you try to reflect as many different points of view as you can, so that students have the opportunity to write and then speak about different ideas concerning the debate. If successful, it might become the main body of a lesson and not just a starter, but you will need to keep a careful eye on it!

Godly play

Godly play is a movement that began with the work of the Rev. Jerome Berryman trying to apply the techniques of Montessori, who had encouraged learning via play. The godly play process has four essential ways of operating:

- Creating a sacred space. Can you create this concept in a secular environment?
- Building and working in the community
- Learning religious language
- Using religious language to make meaning.

In the sessions, there should a prepared space. There should be story telling with the use of artefacts and the students should be free to explore the stories of a religious tradition in a free way.

It is vital that they should also be able to use different media – art, writing, play/role-play – to express their responses. In church sessions, there is always a simple feast (a biscuit and drink) and time for sharing.

Scriptural reasoning

This technique has developed from conversations between members of a faith. When practised outside the classroom, you would perhaps bring a Muslim and Christians to compare/contrast what their scriptures say about a particular theme. (See *How to Pitch a Tent*, by William Taylor, St Ethelburga's Centre for Reconciliation and Peace, 78 Bishopsgate, London EC2N 4AG or at www.scripturalreasoning.org). Why not try this as an activity for some of the more gifted and talented pupils, to compare and contrast scriptures across the traditions? They could also try to get in contact with religious leaders via the internet to help them to develop their thinking.

Silent debate

It is not always easy to get all students involved in debate. Write or type out a statement or a question that you would like them to consider. It could be 'Abortion is always wrong'.

Students then have to write their opinion in a speech bubble, which they then attach to an arrow that joins the statement. When others write their statements, they should try to join any ideas or questions that seem to link together.

These can then be put up on display for students to reflect on and discuss. You might be able to put two or three different questions or statements to be tested so that you can help to develop students' ability to answer questions. This technique will enable students who are naturally a little shyer to feel that they have participated in the lesson and, because they do not have to say who wrote what, it might enable opinions to be discussed that otherwise might be ignored.

This technique is especially useful in Religious Studies, in which there might be believers in the classroom who are a little reticent orally but may find the confidence to express themselves through this method.

Written plenaries

The following are three different types of plenaries that you could use if you were studying the life of Gandhi.

Gandhi binary
Choose one of the words from the pairs and fill in the word you choose in the connected sentence:

1. Brave/cowardly
2. Wise/foolish
3. Humble/arrogant
4. Thoughtful/thoughtless
5. Correct/wrong

1. Gandhi was ... because ...
2. Gandhi was ... because ...
3. Gandhi was ... because ...
4. Gandhi was ... because ...
5. Gandhi was ... because ...

Then answer this question:

> Would the problems of India and South Africa over racism have been much more quickly solved if Gandhi had allowed his followers to use violence?
> Give reasons for your answer, showing that you have thought about it from more than one point of view.

Gandhi Millionaire

This approach uses the techniques of the *Who Wants To Be a Millionaire?* quiz programme. How might you include the idea of phone a friend, ask the audience and fifty/fifty in a classroom context? (* denotes the right answers)

1. Gandhi was born in
   a. 1869 *
   b. 1874
   c. 1879
   d. 1901.

2. Gandhi was thrown off a train in South Africa, as
   a. Indians were not allowed to travel in First Class *
   b. he had made too much noise
   c. he had been rude to the guard
   d. he was not wearing a tie.

3. Gandhi set up an Ashram, which is
   a. a small business
   b. a community of all faiths and races *
   c. a temple
   d. a small statue.

4. Gandhi campaigned against the Pass laws as
   a. they were racist *
   b. he did not like the colour of the pass
   c. he needed something to do
   d. he supported the government.

5. Gandhi believed that, in the Hindu idea of Ahimsa,
   a. you should pray five times a day

    b. you should do no violence to any living thing *

    c. you should try to go on pilgrimage

    d. violence is always acceptable.

6. Gandhi believed that you should show humility. This is
    a. thinking you are better than others
    b. ignoring the needs of others
    c. thinking others are better than you *
    d. thinking about others and yourself with equal respect.

7. Gandhi joined the Congress Party when he returned to India because
    a. they wanted the British to rule India
    b. they wanted a health service
    c. they wanted Indian independence *
    d. they wanted to sell government houses to make money.

8. The Muslim leader of the Congress Party was called
    a. Jinnah *
    b. Gandhi
    c. Nehru
    d. Godse.

9. Gandhi was assassinated by
    a. Nehru
    b. Jinnah
    c. Patel
    d. Godse *

Gandhi Blockbusters

Alternatively, you can use the technique of *Blockbusters*. If you can get the honeycomb board on either a board or on an electronic whiteboard, then it will have much more appeal for students. I will give you two examples of this, to help you to think about how you might use them in your classroom.

Gandhi Blockbusters: Week 1
1. AS – type of community set up by Gandhi (ashram)
2. AH – doing no violence (Ahimsa)
3. SA – country in which Gandhi practised as a lawyer (South Africa)
4. SAT – pursuing truth (Satya)
5. BE – South Africa was part of this (British Empire)
6. GS – name given to Gandhi (Great Soul)
7. MA – name given to Gandhi in Hindi (Mathatma)

8. HU – not being bigheaded (humility)
9. AT – Hindu term for a soul (Atman)
10. BR – Hindu term for God (Brahman)
11. FC – Gandhi was not allowed to travel in this on the train (First Class)
12. PA – documents that all Indians had to carry
13. MAR – law that made only Christian marriages legal in South Africa (Marriages Act)

Gandhi Blockbusters: Week 2
1. VA – a group in society (varna)
2. JA – a name for subgroups in society (jati)
3. CA – another name for a subgroup (caste)
4. UN – the name of the group at the bottom of society (Untouchables)
5. R – name given to the British rule of India (Raj)
6. SOM – part of Jesus' teaching that Gandhi took inspiration from (Sermon on the Mount)
7. NE – first Indian Prime Minister (Nehru)
8. IN – cause Gandhi fought for in India (Independence)
9. CP – political party Gandhi joined (Congress Party)
10. VI – place where Gandhi believed people should live (villages)
11. HI – religion Gandhi belonged to (Hindu)
12. MU – second biggest religious group in India (Muslim)
13. SM – protest led by Gandhi (Salt March)

Students love to be in a competitive situation: here is one that I have tried:

5 to 1

Here is an idea for a plenary and a starter. Start the lesson with ten questions that you ask students to write their answers to in the back of their books. Towards the end of the lesson, give out five cards to selected students, numbered 1 to 5. Ask the students to huddle together and swap cards. Then select at random one of the numbers. You therefore will not be biased in choosing a particular student. Then ask the student the same ten questions that you asked at the beginning of the lesson. When I tried this the first time, a student who had scored 4 out of 10 at the beginning of the lesson had moved up to 9 out of 10!

Match the word

Take in all the textbooks and ask all students to put away their exercise books. Then write up key words with key definitions on the board, but jumble them up. Ask the class how many they think they could get right and then choose one pupil to join the right definitions with the right words.

Pupil questions
Ask pupils to write one question about some topic covered during the lesson. They must put their name on the question. Then choose three students to try to answer at least two each. Try to mix them up so that students do not get the questions they wrote.

Teaching strategies

Alongside the project or the use of textbooks, how else might we get students to learn? The following are a few other suggestions.

Using the board-game approach

Students will be very familiar with the idea of a board game. This can also be a good device to consolidate learning about a particular topic. Here is an example:

Year 8: The Gurus game

You have two weeks and two homeworks to devise a game to explain to a Sikh young person about the importance of the Gurus. You will need to include the following:

- a board
- a set of question cards
- a dice
- a set of instructions
- counters

You can model your game on existing board games, like Trivial Pursuit or Monopoly, but remember that the main aim is to educate about the Gurus. You may work with a partner if you wish. You will have the opportunity to play your games and those of others in a lesson to come.

Top trumps

Ask pupils to create a series of top trumps cards about figures that are important to a religion – such as the ten gurus or the key people mentioned in the stories about the Buddha. You need to include four or five categories. For example:

- name
- age when he died
- method of death
- country of birth
- single/married

Pupils then need to match up or take cards from other people in the room.

Using art

There are many different ways in which you can use art. You might consider making stained-glass windows. You can make artefacts from a religion. You might encourage students to explore the idea of a sacred object by asking them to model in clay an item that they regard as important to them.

Collage is another method by which you could produce a representation of a topic such as racism or poverty or religious diversity.

Writing newspaper articles

Encouraging pupils to develop a newspaper article about a religious theme is one way in which they can think through some of the issues about bias and interpretation in religion.

It is important to set a task to help pupils to develop a whole set of competing versions. After all, the four gospels each give us an account of the death of Jesus, but are often very different about the details. Pupils could be asked to do the following:

- Create a name for your paper.
- Write a bold headline.
- When writing about the death of Jesus, make sure that you report the views of the Christians, the Romans and the Jews. Show a variety of opinions.
- You could write an editorial for your newspaper, trying to look at all the evidence and the opinions about why Jesus was put to death on a cross.

The use of Word might help pupils to create the typeface that looks like a newspaper. Google images or other picture search engines will also help pupils to develop an impressive piece of work.

Writing approaches

1. Write a biography of a religious figure. They have to, in a limited number of words – say 250 words – try to catch the essence of the person's life and teaching. This is a good exercise to help pupils to focus on the most important aspects of a person. You can then ask pupils to read these out and see if there are common threads or obvious omissions. For example, does an obituary of Jesus explain the ideas his disciples have about his rising from the dead or is it too narrowly focused on his moral teaching?
2. Use rap. Pupils can use rap in RE but you must make sure that they do not use racist, sexist, homophobic or obscene language or ideas. Most pupils think they know the structures to writing a rap: only a few can do so successfully but when it is done correctly, then it can produce work that is fun and educational. Make sure, too, that they do more than pastiche their favourite rap track, but should try to develop their own work. Many stories do have a recurring structure that can lend itself to this form, such as the parables of Jesus or a Buddhist tale.
3. Cut-up story. One way of introducing a story to pupils might be to do so using a series of cards with the key parts of the story on them, which are randomly sorted. In small groups, the cards must be rearranged to make sure that the right order is established. This will encourage pupils to think about the importance of the story as a whole and may well help to aid the concentration of the group.
4. Write a postcard-length answer. Tell the pupils that they have precisely 50 words to describe an event or idea (excluding the 'Dear …' greeting at the beginning and the 'Yours, so and so' at the end). You could provide them with plain white postcards, encouraging them to draw a symbol or picture that reflects the content of what they write about on the other side.
5. Letter writing can be a very important way of communication. Within Christianity, the letters of Paul and the other epistle writers as well as the Encyclicals of the Pope have had an enormous impact on how believers think and act.

Some classes may be much more comfortable using an email format. Ask the class whether they think that emails and letters achieve different aims. Can you say things in letters that you cannot in emails and vice versa? Do letters have a more long-term effect than emails? How might religious people use emails effectively?

Some thoughts about groupings

There are many different ways in which you can group pupils in order to work. In lessons, you might well find that you use a variety of groupings during the course:

1. Individually.
2. In pairs.
3. In pairs to begin with, then they join with another pair to develop a theme (which is a technique called snowballing).
4. Groups. Should you let students work in friendship groups? It is good practice to try and make students to work with people who are outside of their friendship group and also to work with those who may be of a different ability, so that we can begin to break down divisions within the class.
5. Whole-class events. How can you manage and sustain these? Some classes will not be able to cope with this approach for a long period of time, whilst others will.

Key Stage 4 RE

Key Stage 4 GCSE/GCSE Short Course/entry level

There are many different routes that you can take with students in Key Stage 4. These include the following:

1. Non-examination RE. This has often been part of a set of modules in PSHE, for example. This has suffered from the problem of trying to get the students motivated or being delivered by less than keen non-specialists. All courses in GCSE Short Courses and Full Courses cited are from September 2009 and will be subject to regular review and/or change.
2. GCSE Religious Studies. The Full Course normally consists of two modules, either two world religions, a world religion and a morality module, or two Christianity courses.
3. GCSE Religious Studies Short Course. This course should be taught for at least 5 per cent of curriculum time in Key Stage 4, which is equivalent to a 1-hour lesson in most schools, looking at issues of morality and ultimate questions, rather than looking at ceremonies or festivals.
4. Entry-level certificate in RE. This enables students who are not highly academic to do a course that can lead to a certificate and is largely project-based.

There are three principal examination bodies – AQA, Edexcel and OCR – that produce these courses. It is very important that you read the specifications carefully, as they will be constantly updated. They are available on their respective websites.

You need to consider how easy these modules are to teach, what resource implications there are and if they are accessible to students. If you decide to change syllabus or board, make sure that you attend a training meeting. It is also useful to try to attend the exam feedback meeting at which examiners give their views on the paper and how candidates performed. This can provide vital insight into how to get candidates in the following year to write better answers that more accurately match the criteria.

Let us look at each of these boards and see what they offer in terms of GCSE – entry-level, Short Course and Full Course GCSE. You might also like to consider entering some of the bright students for A2 papers, either in Religious Studies or Philosophy or Critical Thinking.

The exam boards

AQA is contactable at www.aqa.org.uk, EdExcel can be reached at www.edexcel.org.uk and OCR can be contacted at www.ocr.org.uk. Those in Wales need to contact www.wjec.co.uk and those in Scotland can get information at www.sqa.co.uk. There are details at each of these sites of entry-level, Short and Full Course GCSEs in Religious Studies, which are being constantly updated. Each board also provides training in their exams, normally free of charge to the schools opting for their courses.

Important terms or phrases for GCSE

These are key terms in most RS GCSE courses:

Abortion	Morality
Agnostic	Pacifist
Amoral	Pollution
Atheist	Poverty
Commitment	Prejudice
Conservation	Quality of life
Cosmological argument	Racism
Covenant (in marriage)	Sanctity of life
Design argument	Sexism
Discrimination	Stereotype
Environment	Stewardship
Holy war	Unmerited suffering
Human rights	Vegan
Immoral	Vegetarianism
Just war	Wealth
Merited suffering	

Classroom management

Joining an RE department

Joining an RE department, be it as a PGCE, GTP or newly qualified teacher, can be quite daunting. You may be working either totally by yourself or with a limited number of colleagues. There can be great pressures. Let us examine some case studies of issues that could arise.

If you are already a Head of Department, hopefully the case studies will help you to think about what good practice should be with regards to helping staff.

Case study: Problems with the Head of Department

Jenny started her NQT year in September and, by half-term, she, like many new teachers, was finding things tough. Just after half-term, her Head of Department, Colin, went on long-term sick for over 2 months, leaving Jenny to act as head of department. When Colin returned to school, he was clearly allowing Jenny to make too many decisions. He was quick to ask her for copies of videos or lesson plans or material that she had written, seemingly not producing any of his own.

Jenny is increasingly being perceived by the management as the effective Head of Department, which, while it pleases her ego, she knows is a situation that must create long-term damage to her relationship with Colin.

What should she do and whom should she turn to?

As Jenny is in her NQT year, there should be someone in the school whom she can turn to apart from her Head of

Department. There should be a professional tutor who supervises all the NQTs. She also could talk to the line manager of her Head of Department, probably of Faculty or Team-Leader level. By taking her concerns to this person, she does not necessarily have to confront the Head of Department, but, hopefully, a more experienced colleague may be able to communicate to them in a way that her Head of Department does not find threatening.

Case study: The too busy Head of Department

Andrew has arrived in a department where his Head of Department is also in charge of PSHE, the Assembly rota and the development of Citizenship. The HOD is also on the school governors and is currently undertaking an MA. He has also recently become a father.

Although there is a time-tabled slot for the HOD and Andrew to meet, he frequently cancels these and is often looking at his watch, giving the impression that he is keen to get on with other work. He is also quick to flatter Andrew, to tell him what a wonderful job he is doing and imply that he does not need to give him that much support.

Andrew is actually aware of his shortcomings and, in talking to NQTs in other departments, he does feel that he is not being supported as he should.

What should Andrew do? Does the Head of Department's line manager need to act – if so, how?

Teachers are quite often classic over-committers and this Head of Department is one example, which has consequences not just for Andrew, but for the department. By failing to meet with Andrew, the Head of Department is probably adding to their own stress, let alone Andrew's, as they are failing to pick up on areas in which they could perhaps delegate or work in partnership with him. The line manager of the Head of Department needs to act in order to help the department run smoothly. We need to think about what is a priority and staff induction in their first year, in particular, is a high priority.

The Head of Department also needs to make sure that they get their work in balance and that they learn to prioritize their work into what is urgent (i.e. do today), important (do in the next few days) and a task to do (which might be long-term). It is often tempting to do paperwork rather than look at staff issues, as people-centred work might be open-ended and the paperwork might seem like an achievable goal.

Case study: A good start

Jenny made such a good start, especially with the discipline of her classes, that the Head of Department has assumed that she has very few problems with classes. Few pupils are now sent to the HOD and neither the Patrol nor the Behaviour Support Manager has picked up on any discipline problems. The HOD had previously had a member of staff who had frequently caused unnecessary confrontations with pupils and had overacted in the circumstances.

The HOD and other members of staff have constantly praised Jenny for her discipline but she is beginning to think that she is now unable to share the discipline problems she has. She feels that she might lose face, letting the HOD down, who had such a bad time with the previous member of staff.

Yet, Jenny is finding that many break times and lunchtimes as well as after school are taken up with detentions or writing letters to parents about bad behaviour. A Year 8 class to whom she is teaching Islam (not one of her strengths) have been especially badly behaved, although, when she hinted at this to the HOD, they said 'They have never been a problem for me.' (The HOD is a teacher of 20 years' experience and is a Head of Year.)

What should she do? Who might be able to help her deal with this situation?

The issue is that the Head of Department is being too confident about Jenny's performance and this has the potential to backfire. He or she may well fail to give really comprehensive instructions, thinking that Jenny just understands what to do when she really needs much clearer guidance. This may affect the lesson planning and the pace of the NQT's lessons, which may have a knock-on effect on discipline. There has to be an understanding that the NQT, however confident in manner or in the way they talk about the job, is still a learner and should be treated as such.

The NQT might also be trying to act like a more experienced member of staff and needs to be reassured that, with time, their confidence and understanding of the demands of student behaviour and the curriculum will be dealt with. Even if the Head of Department is a workaholic, they need to make sure that their bad work habits or stress are not passed on. They need to encourage the NQT to rest as well as to work. They need to rightly value the NQT – not over or under. To do that will take time and effort in getting to know them.

Case study: Revealing too much?

Simon was encouraged at his university to think about the way in which he could use his own experiences and beliefs to help pupils to understand. He is naturally the sort of person who reveals a great deal about their inner life.

He has been taking a group of Year 10 pupils. They have been studying Christian teaching on sex before marriage. Simon is single and believes that marriage is the only appropriate context for sexual intercourse.

During a discussion in a lesson, one student asks Simon, 'Sir, you're a Christian. Are you married?' Simon says he is not married. The pupil looks at him and then asks, 'So are you a virgin then?'

How should he answer that question? What problems might there be if he does answer it?

There should be some degree of mystery about a teacher; there needs to be some necessary distance between pupil and teacher in order for there to be discipline and an understanding of who is in charge of the classroom. You also need to consider that what you might say may well be passed on to other conversations that pupils have in their other lessons and that this might make other members of staff uneasy, as they might have pressure to answer personal questions. Whilst, in RE, the personal story or the sharing of belief or experience is important, you need to have in your own mind a line in the sand beyond which you will not go or allow students to question.

Seating plan

With the great throughput of classes, a seating plan is probably more essential in RE than most other lessons, in which higher contact means that the teacher has a chance at instilling discipline more than once a week as well as getting to know the names of all the students and not just the naughty or outstanding ones! As Dietrich Bonhoeffer once wrote, 'Discipline is one of the stations to freedom' – good discipline frees people and classes to be what they could be. It is about meekness. When Jesus says, 'Blessed are the meek', he is using in the word 'meek' a word that refers to using the power of a horse to a good end, breaking its wildness so that it can become useful to others and better controlled.

Discipline should not be primarily about telling off, but leading students to behaving in appropriate and sensible ways that help them and others to learn and to feel safe in your classroom. How can you put this into practice?

It may be the case that there is a school or departmental seating plan to follow. If there isn't, probably the best strategy is to do boy/girl seating. Take into account any major behavioural problems or students with learning difficulties, so you may well break an alphabetical sequence in the way that they are arranged in the class.

Putting them into a seating plan may not make you popular: you will probably be greeted by 'But I want to sit with my friend!' However, the evidence from OFSTED and others who have studied it suggests that this type of plan promotes learning. It has the effect in particular of keeping boys on task as well as removing the issue of dealing with fragile friendships amongst all students that would otherwise lead to problems.

Some flexibility is advised but do not give in to every suggestion, allowing people to move because a pupil isn't there that week and they would like to sit next to their friend.
However, there will be pairings that do not work and you will need to be aware of the possibility and allow some movement.

Leave a seating plan for the supply or cover teacher when you are not in class so that they can be identified and do not wander from their places!

Seating plans send a message about who is in control. Explain the importance of the plan to you and to them. They still may not like it, but they need to learn that they cannot always get what they want so that all might have the right atmosphere for learning.

Controversial issues in classes

As well as dealing with the controversial issues in the syllabus or schemes of work that we are following, RE is likely to be a subject that will raise difficult issues in the way students speak or act.

Dealing with racism

Case study: Silly behaviour

Jenny has a class who think it is amusing to speak in mock Indian accents when they are reading about Hinduism. She is at a loss as to what she should do in order to stop this.

What should she do? The class probably don't realize that they are being offensive. Does this excuse their behaviour?

This sort of behaviour cannot go unchallenged: she has to tackle it and explain to the group that she expects them to show respect. The fake accents are racist and inappropriate. In order to learn respect and appropriate behaviour, students must be told that what they are doing is not acceptable.

Case study: Blasphemy

Andrew is troubled as to how to approach the issue of blasphemy. Many pupils say 'O God' or 'Jesus Christ' when they are talking in a lesson. This is not language that is challenged by other teachers, though the school is very tough on sexual swearing.

He has, on a couple of occasions, challenged pupils about this, pointing out that he finds this offensive, but they look genuinely confused that this is causing him offence.

What should Andrew do? Should the Head of Department get involved and, if so, how? Should the school incorporate new rules about blasphemy?

You cannot necessarily expect other members of staff to go along with you, but, for the RE teacher, it is about respect to faith and communities of believers. It is therefore not inappropriate to set this as a standard in your classroom. RE is about learning to value others and to show respect.

Case study: A pupil takes offence

Chris has a good sense of humour but, in one of his lessons, he made a joke at a female pupil's expense, which she took as a criticism of her religion, which led her to walk out of his lesson in tears. He went to apologize but although the pupil seemed to accept this, he has noticed that she seems angry around him.

Should he tell his Head of Department? Should he talk to the pupil's parents to avoid misunderstanding?

This is a situation that needs careful handling. Chris should tell the Head of Department and write down exactly what happened, so that rumour or exaggeration cannot happen. In the most serious cases, contacting the parents would be wise, so that the heat can be taken out of the situation. It is important that we think very carefully about the language we use to students.

Using students' faith

It is vital that all students regard your classroom as a safe place. There is a temptation to use students whom you know practise a faith – especially a minority one – to act as unpaid experts for you. This is very dangerous. For teenagers, coming to a sense of confidence about their faith might well be a struggle. They might feel unable to express what they might want to say about their faith, as they are only beginning to internalize, to make it personal. They might be going another way – perhaps away from personal belief – yet they might be unhappy to show that for fear of upsetting members of their community.

It may be that some members of a faith are willing to speak. Be careful – the teenage years can be a time of extremes and they therefore might not accurately represent the religion they belong to. They might not also show the understanding of others and self-reflection that should categorize the use of the faith in RE.

Similarly, be careful about using a parent of a class member as an expert if you get someone in. This can be embarrassing or difficult for both parents and children. Try to avoid using a parent with the class that a child might be in and, if you can, avoid the year group to which they belong.

Assessment and reporting

Assessment

Assessment is always difficult for RE teachers, especially as the sheer throughput of pupils is enormous. In many schools, RE departments are two-people departments, with possibly only Drama or Music being of a similar size, but both of those latter departments are much less likely to have the amount of contact that RE has with Key Stage 4.

The RE department will have a number of different ways to assess pupil progress. These will include:

Class work
Homework
Tests
Project-based work
Exams
Oral responses in class through questioning or discussion.

Oral-feedback assessment

A great deal of what a teacher does in terms of assessment is to give oral feedback. We use this because it can:

- be immediate
- be personal
- be two-way
- enable explanations to be checked
- be helpful
- give an impact that affects the pupil.

Oral feedback tends to be instant and sometimes, as a consequence, not well thought-out. Why not experiment in writing some notes so that when you have that minute or so talking to a pupil, then you make it as useful as it can be?

We should keep focusing on the targets, the standards and levels that we think the student is capable of delivering. We should also use it to help students to clarify issues that might slow their learning and to help them to identify the next stages in their development.

We spend a great deal of time on feedback: it can be a very important route to improving student performance.

It is key that pupils receive assessment that requires them to learn about religion (knowledge/understanding tasks) and learn from religion (evaluation, explaining their own viewpoints). These enable us to be able to make judgements about students' ability to understand, their knowledge and their ability to evaluate ideas as well as to develop their own beliefs.

Peer and self-assessment

DJ Simon Mayo asked people to email his programme with ideas that people use to help reduce their workload. A primary-school teacher replied that she 'got the pupils to do peer assessment as this saved her doing a lot of marking at home after the end of the school day'. It is not going to be that easy, I'm afraid! It will require planning and thought if it is to be successful.

Peer assessment encourages students to assess their peers' work and to make constructive criticisms in order to help them develop. For example, you might ask a group to do an exam question like this:

> Animal rights should be the same as human rights' What do you think? How might Christians answer this? Show that you have thought about it from more than one point of view. Remember to include religious teachings and beliefs in your answer.

In order for students to do this effectively, you should give them either:

1. Criteria that explain how a pupil gets a good grade. In Key Stage 3, you can use levels. In Key Stage 4, you could look at these grade descriptions from AQA's GCSE Short Course. Here are some criteria used by one exam board – AQA – to help give grade boundaries:

   > Grade A candidates demonstrate detailed and comprehensive knowledge and understanding of beliefs, values and traditions and their impact on the lives of individuals,

societies and cultures. They do this by consistently using and interpreting a range of specialist vocabulary, drawing out and explaining the meaning and religious significance of the religion(s) studied and explaining, where appropriate, how differences in belief lead to differences of religious response. They support, interpret and evaluate a variety of responses recognizing the complexity of issues, weighing up opinions and by making judgements supported by a range of evidence and well-developed arguments.

Grade C candidates demonstrate, generally with accuracy, a knowledge and understanding of beliefs, values and traditions and their impact on individuals, societies and cultures. They do this by using correct specialist vocabulary when questions specifically demand it and describing accurately and explaining the importance of the religion(s) studied. They support, interpret and evaluate different responses to issues studied by presenting relevant evidence to support arguments, incorporating reference to different points of view and using arguments to make reasoned judgements.

Grade F candidates demonstrate elementary knowledge and understanding of beliefs, values and traditions studied and their impact on adherents and others. They do this through limited use of specialist vocabulary and knowledge, sometimes correctly but not often systematically, and by making simple connections between religion and people's lives. They support and evaluate responses to issues studied by giving a reason in support of an opinion.

2. Give students a set of examples of how previous students answer the question, making sure that you remove the names of the students involved. This will give them an idea of how much they need to write and the sort of style they need to adopt in order to get the best grades.
3. You should try to have an oral feedback session, listening to some of the different grades and how the students reached that conclusion. Make sure that you use a variety of different students, all the way across the ability range.

One model for assessment of Key Stage 3

The increasing move towards levelling work from Level 3 at the beginning of Year 7 for the least able to above Level 8 can be a good focus for developing attainment. On a week-by-week basis, other models could be used to help to assess, such as judgements based on attainment and effort.

Attainment
This is graded 1 to 4:

1 = Excellent attainment of Level 5 in Y7, Level 5:3 in Y8, Level 6:1 in Y9
2 = Good attainment of Level 4 in Y7, Level 5 in Y8, Level 5:3 in Y9
3 = Average attainment of Level 3 in Y7, Level 4 in Y8, Level 4:3 in Y9
4 = Below average attainment of Level 3 in Y7, Level 3 by the end of Key Stage 3

Effort
This is graded A to D:

A = Excellent effort
B = Good effort
C = Average effort
D = Below average effort

If no work has been completed, you cannot assess either effort or attainment; therefore, write a U, which stands for unacceptable effort and attainment. Normally, a U should trigger a sanction such as a detention or telling the pupil to complete it for extra homework. Where it is a recurring pattern of three times in a row, the pupil should see the Head of Faculty and a letter should be sent home.

These gradings should apply to the class and homework produced. For more extended pieces of homework, over a number of weeks, levelling is advised, as the length of a task set should enable accurate levelling to be achieved.

Project work can be marked using these grades, but, as projects could provide useful information about the level that pupils are working towards, it might be sensible to mark in levels.

This example on the Gurdwara gives an indication of how levelling can be applied to projects. You may well want to divide the levels into sub-levels to help with assessment, to show pupils whether they are just on the level, safely on the level or above the average of the level.

A visit to the Gurdwara

You must write a detailed account of what you would find in a Gurdwara, the Sikh place of worship. You should:

1. Explain what the word 'Gurdwara' means.
2. Explain what the Khanda and Nishan Sahib are.
3. Describe what you would see when you go into a Gurdwara and the Langar.
4. Explain the following words and what they have to do with the Gurdwara:

   Takht
   Palki
   Granthi
   Guru Granth Sahib
   Giannis
   Chauri
   Diwan
   Ragis
   Karah Parshad

5. Explain how the Gurdwara and the Langar show the Sikh belief that all people are equal and should be treated with respect.
6. If you have time, include some drawings/diagrams for things you might see in a Gurdwara. Make sure that these are labelled appropriately.

In the Gurdwara project, pupils will need to do the following to achieve these levels:

Level 3 pupils will give simple explanations of key words and ideas. They will attempt to answer all questions, but their answers, especially those that are linked to developing their own viewpoints, lack depth. They may include some diagrams, but these will not include as much information as they should.

Level 4 pupils will give good explanations of key words and terms. They will attempt to answer all questions and will be strong in answering matters of knowledge but will lack depth on questions of understanding and developing their own viewpoints. They will include some diagrams that will be labelled and explained to a good standard.

Level 5 pupils will give full explanations of key words and terms. They will answer all questions, giving developed answers in questions of knowledge, understanding and developing their own viewpoints. They will add to their work with clearly labelled pictures and diagrams to an excellent standard.

Another method of assessment

Another method of assessment that is useful and may prove quicker than the one outlined is based on the levels. With most schools reporting in levels and sub-levels, why not use these to help to inform and develop assessment?

OFSTED are keen for every child to know their level and the steps they need to take to attain progression to the next sub-level or level. One way to do this is to have a form like the example shown that you can stick into a pupil's book.

Levels in Year	What you can do to raise your level
Autumn level	
Spring level	
Summer level	

In this, you mark the level as well as work out with the pupils what they will need to raise their level to the next one. This allows focus and makes it less impersonal than a general marking system. The aim should be to get the pupil to develop, as they should not be obsessed with the marks that others are getting. Each pupil is an individual and, often, assessment systems fall apart, as they do not take sufficient time to deal with this, as the RE teacher is often the one with the most amount of work to mark, which can lead to somewhat impersonal and burdensome assessment that can actually be not fit for purpose.

Rather than mark for attainment or level, you can mark them against the criteria of whether they are on level, above level or below level. One suggestion to show this is to use appropriate pointing arrows, as shown.

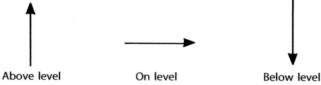

| Above level | On level | Below level |

The focus for your comments then becomes the skills that they need to develop in RE, not the issues that have tended to distract us, such as grammar or spelling. It also avoids the confusion of having one assessment scheme for levelling and one for general classroom practice.

Tests in Key Stage 3

Formal moments of testing are vital in both Key Stages. Try to devise a test that covers the scheme of work that you are teaching. If you have your test on computer, you can then add and delete questions as you try them out on students. Tests should seek to test not just knowledge, but also understanding and the ability of pupils. I have tried to devise tests that are not completely about writing, have a variety of different literacy techniques and use visual techniques. It is important that you have somewhere in a Key Stage 3 test a question that could be in a GCSE paper, as this will help in the identification of the gifted and talented. Here is one example that you could use with a Year 9 project on Martin Luther King:

> 'True peace is not the absence of tension; it is the presence of justice' (Martin Luther King). What does this mean? Do you agree? What do you think King meant by justice? Can it be achieved? What do you think? Give reasons for your answer, showing that you have though about it from more than one point of view.

Here are two examples for you to think about:

Year 7 Christianity Test
Answer all the questions on the paper.

1. Match the right word to the right meaning:
   Pulpit   Place to read the Bible from
   Lectern   A type of seat used in church
   Pew   A place from where a sermon is given

   3 marks

2. Which of the following encouraged Romans to become Christians? Choose either A, B or C:
   A. Augustine
   B. Nero
   C. Constantine

   Answer ....

   1 mark

3. Give two examples of miracles performed by Jesus:

   a.

   b.

2 marks

4. Give three things that could have happened to Jesus if he did not (as Christians believe) come back from the dead:

   a.

   b.

   c.

3 marks

5. 'The stories in the Bible are irrelevant to people today.' What would a Christian say to this? What do you think? Give reasons for your answer, showing that you have thought about it from more than one point of view.

6 marks

6. Give two reasons why pupils need to study Christianity in RE:

   a.

   b.

2 marks

7. Complete the following piece of writing, using the right words, which are below the text:

   > Paul was on his way to .... to arrest .... On the way there, a bright .... appeared in the sky and he heard a voice asking him why he was persecuting him. Paul asked the

voice who he was, and the voice replied, 'I am.............' Paul was .... for a few days and had to be led into the city of Damascus. While there, he was baptised and soon began to speak about his faith in Jesus. He had to escape from the city as his .... was threatened by people angry that he had changed his beliefs.

Words: Christians   Damascus   light   Paul   blind   life

5 marks

8. Complete the following piece of writing, using the words below:

   Jesus told stories known as .... One of the most famous is the .... Samaritan, in which an enemy of the .... people is one who helps a person in need.

   Words: Jewish   parables   good

3 marks

Sikhism Test
Answer all the questions on the paper.

1. The word Guru means (choose either A or B):

   A. teacher
   B. guide

      Answer ....

1 mark

2. The founder of Sikhism was (choose either A or B):

   A. Guru Nanak
   B. Guru Gobind Singh

      Answer ....

1 mark

3. What was the importance of a circle of golden light appearing around the head of Guru Nanak at his birth?

2 marks

4. Fill in the missing gaps, using some of the words below:

   Guru Nanak was born into a .... family. He had friends
   who were both Hindus and .... When he was ....,
   he believed that he was taken up to .... where God
   himself appeared to him. Then Guru Nanak began to travel
   around .... and he began to gain followers who were
   called Sikhs, which means ....

   Words: Disciples 30 India Hindu Muslims Heaven

   6 marks

5. Draw and label three of the five Ks.

   3 marks

6. What are the Gurdwara and the Langer? Explain what goes on in
   each.

   4 marks

7. How many Sikh gurus were there? (choose either A or B)

   A. 12
   B. 10

   Answer ....

   1 mark

8. Why do men and women sit separately in some Gurdwaras?

   2 marks

9. 'The stories about Guru Nanak have no relevance to the world we live in'. What might a Sikh say in reply to this? What do you think? Show that you have thought about it from two different points of view.

5 marks

The examples I have given are all out of 25 marks: four a year could be used to add up to a full test or examination in Key Stage 3.

Tests should be out of 25. I then suggest that you can analyse pupils' levels in the following ways.

In Years 7 and 8, the following grade boundaries could be set:

1–3	Level 3:c
4–6	Level 3:b
7–8	Level 3:a
9–13	Level 4:c
14–16	Level 4:b
17–19	Level 4:a
20–22	Level 5:c
23–24	Level 5:b
25	Level 5:a

In Year 7, no level higher than 5:c should normally be awarded (there may be an extremely bright pupil, but check with Head of Faculty before awarding the level). In Year 8, a top pupil can score level 6:c; anything above, again please consult. In Year 9, the gradings for levels are:

1–3	Level 3:c
4–6	Level 3:b
7–8	Level 3:a
9–11	Level 4:c
12–13	Level 4:b
14–15	Level 4:a
16–18	Level 5:c
19–21	Level 5:b
22–23	Level 5:a
24–25	Level 6:c

Most pupils at the end of Key Stage 3 should be 5–6. It may be that pupils over-perform or under-perform in tests, so please also use other data. Pupils who consistently obtain 1A in their class and homework as well as tests and projects should be given the highest levels. We need to be able to show both continuity and progression through the levels, in a clear and sensible way.

Pupil-friendly levels

It is good practice to give pupils a sense of what each level is in language that they can relate to. Here are some models – I have selected levels 3, 5 and 8 to show you the range in Key Stage 3. You might also like to consider how you might write into levels more understanding of skills that they need to develop. The brave might also develop these into sub-levels!

> Level 3: I am able to give brief explanations of key religious words and ideas. I attempt to answer most questions, writing answers that briefly cover the topic. I include some diagrams but with brief or few explanations.

> Level 6: I am able to give fairly full explanations of key religious words and ideas. I am able to answer all questions and am especially strong on knowledge-based questions. I show good ability in answering those that test understanding. I am developing the skill to answer longer answers that test understanding. I am growing in confidence to express my own point of view as well as showing some understanding of alternatives to that. When I include diagrams, they are clearly labelled and explained to a very good standard.

> Level 8: I am able to give full explanations of key religious words and ideas. I answer all questions and am strong in answering matters of knowledge. I also have developed longer answers that show good understanding. I can develop full answers that reflect my own point of view. I am able to fully consider the strengths and weakness of both my own and others' arguments. When I include diagrams, they are to labelled and explained to an excellent standard.

GCSE assessment

The GCSE short-course grades set by AQA will provide us with an example of exam assessment:

A*	90%
A	80%
B	70%
C	60%
D	50%
E	40%
F	30%
G	20%
U	Below 20%

For mock exams, you might well try to show students what they need to achieve in order to gain the best grade. As a mock can take place 5–6 months before the examination, you can slightly scale the marks down, but you must explain to students that they will need to achieve more:

A*	85%
A	75%
B	65%
C	55%
D	45%
E	35%
F	28%
G	20%
U	Below 20%

Hopefully, this will mean that we will encourage pupils and help them to see the possible room for improvement that they can make between the mock and the actual exam. A few weeks after the mock, it is a good idea to begin to make pupils aware of the marking scheme of the exam, so that they do not assume that little revision can get them a good pass at GCSE!

Try to mark using notes reflecting effort and use exam-like essay questions to assess them in a way that will help them to see the skills that they will need to develop to reach the best grades in the examination. On reports, the exam grade given reflects the grade given in the mock or Year 10 exam. The potential exam grade should reflect the mock grade and the general standard or the known ability of the pupil.

In assessing in Key Stage 4, it is vital that you think about how much evidence the pupil shows in:

1. Knowledge – do they know the key ideas/facts?
2. Understanding – do they understand and explain the key ideas? Can they see a link between belief and behaviour?

3. Evaluation – are they able to develop their own ideas with reference to religious ideas?

There are dilemmas when it comes to marking exams. Think about the case study that follows.

Case study: Exam marking

At the end of the first term, Year 11 had a mock. Duncan was not given the paper by his Head of Department until the day before. He was not given a detailed marking scheme and is struggling to understand how to mark the paper and what grades/percentages he should award.

The Head of Department is a senior examiner for a board and seems to assume that Duncan will have been taught to mark exams as part of his university training or when he was doing his placements. Duncan also has twice as many papers to mark as the Head of Department, and then will be expected to write detailed reports of pupils whom he has only taught for the majority of the autumn term.

What should Duncan do? How can the Head of Department help Duncan to cope with large amount of marking and report writing?

Duncan must feel secure in marking papers and time has to be given to talking him through the process. Giving him a typed marking scheme will help, but this will often need to be carefully explained and applied to an exam paper in order to do things effectively. It is a temptation of the Head of Department to think that things are clear when they might not necessarily be so: spending time with the NQT will help to avoid this problem.

All teachers want their students to succeed – how far should we try to make them succeed against the odds? Think about the following case study.

Case study: Marking to encourage

Chris has been given a GCSE group that contains a pupil called Jill. She has worked hard in lessons and normally achieves good grades. The school predicts that she is the type of pupil who should get a grade B in the final exam.

Although it is evident from the mock that Jill has tried hard and shows that revision was done, her score is in the E boundary. Chris is tempted to mark her paper a second time, trying to give her a better mark.

Should he do this? How might he be able to encourage Jill, even if he decides that the E mark will have to remain?

Marking to encourage is often highly counterproductive, as it will give both the parent and the pupil an unrealistic view of their progress. Is it done from a genuine desire to encourage the pupil or is it done so that the teacher can reward a pupil that he or she finds personally agreeable? We should try to be fair and accurate, whatever our feelings. We cannot nor should not hide pupils from failure: we all learn from failure, quite often more than we do from success!

Open-ended assessment in RE?

Trying to find new methods of assessment that get beyond the superficial can be difficult. The best assessment in RE should be making sure that students have a good grasp of facts, but they also can explain them and use them to develop arguments about religious issues. Following is a template of an assessment I used on a Year 8 class. I started with a pair of contrasting words, asking students to pick the appropriate one of the pair in their opinion. They then had to incorporate that word into a sentence and explain why they were using the word that they did. This technique also revealed to me the students who needed more help, as they did get the meaning of the story wrong (we were studying the story of Abraham, particularly focusing on the near sacrifice of Isaac). I have included a version of this assessment with regards to Gandhi later on in the book.

Abraham

Look at the following pairs of words that could be used about Abraham. Choose one of each set, then fill in the sentences below:

1. wise/foolish

2. brave/cowardly

3. hero/villain

4. loving/unloving

5. thoughtful/too quick to action

Sentences:

1. Abraham was .... because he ....

2. Abraham was .... because he ....

3. Abraham was .... because he ....

4. Abraham was .... because he ....

5. Abraham was .... because he ....

So, in your opinion, was Abraham ultimately a hero, a villain or a bit of both? Give reasons for your answer.

Some of the responses I got included:

> Abraham was wise as he listened to God.
> Abraham was foolish because he was going to kill his son.
> Abraham was loving because he did not want to kill his son.
> Abraham was unloving because he was willing to take the life of his son for God.

A couple of answers to the last question about whether he was a hero or a villain particularly stood out:

> In my opinion, Abraham was neither villain nor hero. He was prepared to kill his son even though he loved him. But he was brave at the same time because giving up his son is the hardest thing he could have done.

> A hero because he didn't kill people only animals and listened to the
> voice of the angel before doing anything else.

This method is particularly good when you are dealing with a lesson that focuses on a religious individual, be they Abraham or Guru Nanak, though you may need to be especially sensitive to religious believers in your classes who might find these contrasts difficult.

RE needs to make sure that questions used for assessment have a good mixture of both open and closed questions, as this reflects the nature of the religious quest, which is often much more open and provisional than some religious people (and teachers!) often admit.

Another example of open-ended assessment follows:

The Passover Story Assessment

Link the following words. Connections can go in any direction but join them with a line and explain the connection that they have with each other:

MOSES

EXODUS   PASSOVER

ANGEL OF DEATH   SEDER PLATE

PLAGUES   SLAVERY

LIBERATION

Other methods of assessment – attitude to learning surveys

As well as the formal testing of learning, it is important to have an understanding of what the attitude to learning might be and how that might affect performance. An example of an attitude to a learning survey that you could carry out with classes in order to see how far learning is progressing is shown. You might also want to add some qualities you would like to see in an RE learner – should there be a judgement made on the tolerance or the respect shown by the learner? Personally, I think that might prove difficult but you are the best person to judge what might work in your assessment of your classes.

Grade	Adjective	Typical student behaviour
1	Outstanding	☐ always punctual to lessons ☐ always attentive when teacher or others are talking ☐ always stays on task, working with a quiet and determined way ☐ always asks questions if in difficulty ☐ always willing to answer questions during whole class teaching, frequently putting up hands
2	Very Good	☐ always punctual to lessons ☐ attentive to teacher or peer talk ☐ always on task, so that work set is usually completed within time allocated ☐ will question if in difficulty ☐ prepared to answer questions and contribute to discussions
3	Good	☐ usually punctual to lessons ☐ mostly attentive to teacher or peer talk ☐ mostly on task, so that work set is often completed within time allocated ☐ will usually question if in difficulty ☐ sometimes prepared to answer questions and contribute to discussions
4	Satisfactory	☐ usually punctual to lessons ☐ usually attentive to teacher or peer talk

Grade	Adjective	Typical student behaviour
		☐ sometimes needs reminding to stay on task, so that there are times when work needs to be completed quicker
		☐ will sometimes question if in difficulty
		☐ will answer questions and contribute to discussions when asked by teacher, and will occasionally put up hand
5	Unsatisfactory	☐ sometimes late to lessons
		☐ sometimes inattentive to teacher or peer talk
		☐ often off task, so that work set is often not completed within time allocated
		☐ reluctant to question if in difficulty, preferring to do nothing
		☐ rarely prepared to answer questions or contribute to discussions
		☐ low level disruption to lessons will prevent other students from effectively learning
		☐ will not respond to classroom teacher intervention to modify behaviour
6	Poor	☐ often late to lessons
		☐ inattentive to teacher or peer talk
		☐ rarely on task, so that work set is usually not completed
		☐ will not question if in difficulty
		☐ not prepared to answer questions nor contribute to discussions
		☐ presents serious disruption to lessons and does not respond to more senior staff or patrol intervention

Writing reports

The sheer volume of the number of reports can be daunting for an RE teacher. For one year group, I had to write 145 reports! It is therefore important that you have a reporting system that you can manage and that is also educationally sound.

Too often, with such numbers, it is difficult to write personal comments apart from about those who are the obvious 'pleasure to teach' or those who are painful to teach. We need to be judging students' academic performance, so I have moved from writing reports to using a spreadsheet. On that, I enter the level (in Key Stage 3) or the exam grade (in Key Stage 4) that the student is at. This is linked to a set of statement banks. I also have a series of tick-boxes to assess them in the following areas: class work, homework, discussion and behaviour/concentration.

By having standard comments, you may well miss out on the personal but you are giving the parents and the student an insight into how they have been performing and giving them advice as to how to make progress in the future.

The report should also have a brief summary of the topics studied by students, which is important, as it will enable parents to see the diversity of what is now taught as RE.

Standard comments for Key Stage 3 RE

Following are some examples of how you could write standard comments (developed from suggestions by Lat Blaylock). I have included comments for levels 3, 5 and 7c to give you an insight into what can be written. You may need to develop a set of criteria that reflects your own school's concerns.

3:c <Name> is able to describe a few key features of religions, recognizing some differences and similarities between them. Some ability to make links between beliefs and the impact religion has on believers' lives has been shown.

<Name> is able to make simple connections with aspects of their own and others' experiences. Some understanding of the importance of values and commitments has been demonstrated, but this needs to be much more fully developed. More regular assistance needs to be asked for to help improve written work. Revision for tests also needs to be much more thorough. Presentation needs to be urgently addressed.

3:b   <Name> is able to describe some key features of religions, recognizing differences and similarities between them. Ability to make links between beliefs and the impact religion has on believers' lives has been shown.

     <Name> is able to make a few straightforward connections with aspects of their own and others' experiences. Some understanding of the importance of values and commitments has been demonstrated, but this needs to be more fully developed. Answers need to be contained in full sentences. Revision for tests also needs to be much more thorough. Presentation of work also needs to be addressed.

3:a   <Name> is able to describe some key features of religions, recognizing differences and similarities between them. Ability to make limited links between beliefs and the impact religion has on believers' lives has been shown.

     <Name> is able to make some more complex connections with aspects of their own and others' experiences. Understanding of the importance of values and commitments has been demonstrated, but this needs to be more fully developed. Answers are sometimes expressed in full sentences, but would be improved by always being so. Revision for tests also needs to be much more thorough. Improvement in presentation is also required.

5:c   <Name> uses an increasingly wide vocabulary to explain the impact of beliefs upon individuals and communities. Some developed answers in these areas have been shown in written work.

     <Name> is able to describe why people belong to religions as well as knowing that similarities and differences illustrate distinctive beliefs within and between religions.

     <Name> is able to explain how religious sources are used to provide answers to ultimate questions and ethical issues. A few examples of diversity within and between religions have been demonstrated.

     <Name> can pose and suggest a few answers to questions of identity, belonging, meaning, purpose, truth, values and commitments, relating these to their own and others' experiences. <Name> can give limited explanations of what influences them, expressing their own and other's views on the challenges of belonging to a religion. Attention should be given to developing this area both in discussion and in written work. Test scores are mostly good, but could be raised by more thorough revision.

5:b   <Name> uses an increasingly wide vocabulary to explain the impact of beliefs upon individuals and communities. Increasing confidence in being able to understand and explain the influence of beliefs has been shown.

      <Name> is able to explain how religious sources are used to provide answers to ultimate questions and ethical issues. A number of examples of diversity within and between religions have been demonstrated.

      <Name> can pose and suggest a number of answers to questions of identity, belonging, meaning, purpose, truth, values and commitments, relating these to their own and others' experiences. Producing more developed written answers should now be the focus for progression.

5:a   <Name> uses an increasingly wide vocabulary to explain the impact of beliefs upon individuals and communities. Confidence in understanding and explaining differences between and within religions has been shown.

      <Name> is able to explain how religious sources are used to provide answers to ultimate questions and ethical issues. <Name> can pose and suggest a number of answers to questions of identity, belonging, meaning, purpose, truth, values and commitments, relating these to their own and others' experiences.

      Mature and thoughtful answers to questions of identity, belonging, meaning, purpose, truth, values and commitments have been demonstrated. These should be shared with others by increasing contributions to class discussion. Test scores are consistently good and revision should continue to be thorough to maintain this standard.

7:c   <Name> uses religious and philosophical vocabulary to give a coherent understanding of religions and beliefs, explaining the reasons for diversity within and between them with assured confidence.

      <Name> is able to analyse why the impact of religions and beliefs on societies and individuals varies. <Name> shows a developed ability to interpret the reasons why different religious traditions provide different answers to ultimate and ethical questions. Some account of the influence of history and culture on aspects of religious life and practice has been exhibited.

      <Name> has exhibited mature use of reasoning and example to express insight into questions of identity, belonging, meaning, purpose, truth, values and commitments relating these to their own and others' experiences. Thoughtful evaluation of these ideas has been demonstrated.

<Name> has considered the challenges of belonging to a religion in the contemporary world, showing some focus on the importance of values and commitments with empathy and understanding. There is evidence of using appropriate evidence and examples to evaluate ultimate and ethical questions. Test scores are consistently excellent and revision should continue to be thorough to maintain this standard.

Statements for GCSE candidates' reports

Statement banks for RE Key Stage 4 – the following statements reflect the grades at GCSE and the comments are influenced by the advice of the exam boards that they give to teachers about grades:

A*/A <Name> has shown a thorough understanding of religious beliefs, how they affect believers and have shown excellent skills in developing personal arguments as well as sensitivity to the ideas of others. <Name> has been well behaved, shown excellent concentration and has scored excellent results in test and exams. Well done! <Name> should make sure that written answers reflect a diversity of opinion, and that they develop critical reflection of the issues being examined.

B <Name> has shown a very good understanding of religious beliefs and how they affect believers and increasingly exhibits the ability to present personal opinions and arguments and shows sensitivity to others.

<Name> has been well behaved, shown good concentration and has produced very good results in their tests and exams.

<Name> could improve these good results by developing answers further. Well done!

C <Name> has shown a good understanding of religious beliefs, how they affect believers and have begun to show increasing skill in developing arguments that are sensitive to the ideas of others.

<Name> has been well behaved, shown good concentration in most lessons and has produced good results in test and exams. Occasionally, written answers need to be developed by writing more complex sentences.

D <Name> has exhibited a fair understanding of religious beliefs, how they affect believers and has begun to show some skill in developing arguments as well as sensitivity to the ideas of others.

<Name> does need to focus on these as areas of development in order to achieve full potential.

<Name> has been well behaved, shown some focus in most lessons and has produced some respectable results in test and exams. Occasionally, written answers need to be developed by writing more complex sentences.

<Name> needs to ask for help more often if the tasks set are not fully understood.

E   <Name> has exhibited some understanding of religious beliefs, how they affect believers and has begun to show some skill in developing arguments as well as sensitivity to the ideas of others.

<Name> does need to focus on these as areas of development in order to achieve full potential.

<Name> has shown some focus in most lessons and has produced some respectable results in test and exams. Occasionally, written answers need to be developed by writing more complex sentences.

<Name> often needs to ask for help more often if the tasks set are not fully understood.

F   <Name> has exhibited limited understanding of religious beliefs, how they affect believers and has begun to show some skill in developing arguments as well as sensitivity to the ideas of others.

<Name> does need to focus on these as areas of development in order to achieve full potential.

<Name> has shown some focus in most lessons. The result of this has is seen in the limited results produced in test and exams. Written answers need to be developed by writing more complex sentences.

<Name> needs to ask for help more often if the tasks set are not fully understood.

G   <Name> has exhibited a very limited understanding of religious beliefs, how they affect believers and has begun to show some skill in developing arguments as well as sensitivity to the ideas of others.

<Name> does need to focus on these as areas of development in order to raise achievement levels and generate an appropriate set of results.

<Name>'s lack of focus in lessons and has produced very limited results in test and exams. Written answers need to be developed by writing more complex sentences.

<Name> needs to ask for help more often if the tasks set are not fully understood.

U   <Name> has exhibited on only a few occasions understanding of religious beliefs, how they affect believers and has begun to show a little skill in developing arguments as well as sensitivity to the ideas of others.

<Name> does need to focus on these as areas of development in order to raise achievement levels and generate an appropriate set of results.

<Name>'s lack of focus in lessons and has produced less than satisfactory results in test and exams. More effort is required to answer questions fully and write more complex sentences.

<Name> needs to stay on task and ask for help more often if the tasks set are not fully understood.

Homework

Homework can be a major issue for an RE teacher. On a twenty-five period, one-hour-a-lesson structure, you could see 17–19 groups. Compare this with your Maths or English colleagues, who would see something between a half and a third of that number. You would have to be a genius of organization in order to keep up with all of that! Such frequency can lead to many headaches!

There is a danger of either not setting homework, setting too much or not setting appropriate homework. A colleague was once horrified by a non-specialist asking a group of Year 7s to write the story of the near sacrifice of Isaac by Abraham from the point of view of the ram!

The key question about homework has to be – does it stretch and develop the students' knowledge of the subject? Or is it just ticking the boxes to keep senior management and parents off our backs? Homework that is just set for the sake of setting it will ultimately prove unproductive and may well lead to pupils having more negative perceptions of the subject than they would otherwise have.

So how can you devise a way to set meaningful homework that benefits students and helps the teacher to manage their workload? One approach is to develop project-based homework, in which pupils are expected to research a topic for 4 or 5 weeks and then submit. Here are three examples that I have used at Key Stage 3. They are not perfect and they are not offered as that: but how might you develop an approach to your situation that encourages students to be independent learners and develops their understanding of the subject?

Year 7: Your Creation Story

You must write and draw a creation story about a world and a universe came into existence – it can be the one we are in or another one that you have made up. In this story, you should do the following:

a. Explain how your world/universe came into existence. Was there a God/Gods/other types of beings involved?
b. Does the world/universe have a purpose, a meaning? If it does, what is it?
c. Creation stories often try to explain why there is pain and evil in the world. You must try to explain this.

Your creation story must include some labelled drawings or diagrams related to the story. If you want to use a computer to help you, you can. If you would prefer it, you can do a storyboard and below are some sentence beginnings to help you get going if you choose this method:

My world/universe was created by …
The first thing to be created was …
The last thing to be created was …
The meaning of the world/universe I created is …
There is pain in my world/universe because …
Evil things happen in my world/universe because …

This homework begins on .... and must be handed in by ....

Year 8 homework project: The Punjab

You must produce a mini-project about the Punjab, the area in India/Pakistan where Sikhism began. You have to find out about the following:

a. The geography of the area – include a map with labels, preferably hand drawn.
b. Find out the major industries in the area.
c. What religions, including Sikhism, are there?
d. Write about the history of the area.
e. Find examples of the Punjabi language and copy them.
f. Include anything else you think is important about the area.
g. Then answer this question: 'I would/would not like to visit the Punjab because …' Try and include three reasons why you would/would not visit the area and explain them in full sentences.

Year 9 Project on Gandhi

This project will take four homeworks and will be handed in on
....

1. Research the life of Gandhi and produce a detailed timeline of his life, including relevant pictures.
2. Find out and explain why the following have links with Gandhi. You will need to write at least two paragraphs for each of these topics:

   a. The Caste System and why Gandhi did not approve of it
   b. Nehru
   c. Jesus' Sermon on the Mount in Matthew's Gospel Chapters 5 to 7
   d. Martin Luther King
3. 'Gandhi's life was spent campaigning against violence, yet he died a violent death. His life was therefore pointless.' What might a follower of Gandhi say? What do you think? Give reasons for your answer, showing that you have thought about it from more than one point of view.

Good project work should make sure that there are questions that address issues of knowledge and understanding, but you should also try to have questions that reflect the ability of the child by including evaluative ones. Once you have a template on your computer, then you will be able to develop variants, so that students of different abilities can be challenged and make progress in line with the expectations that exist for them.

Two projects a term will satisfy parents, especially if they are 3–5 weeks in duration. They will also release you from weekly collecting and marking homework.

These extended pieces of writing will also give pupils the opportunity to develop their ICT skills and independent learning. Make sure that you design projects that can simply allow a student to cut and paste from a website. You will need careful co-ordination with other subjects, so that students are not over-burdened at any one time if other departments are doing their projects.

Projects should also allow you more time to look at the skills that a student is developing or needs help to. Too often, class work is somewhat short and rigorous assessment is not always possible. The project will give you opportunity to encourage self and peer assessment. As you build up a collection of completed projects over the years, it will be possible for students to look at exemplars of projects to help them see how they could improve (make sure that they don't steal the project and then try to pass it off as their own!).

When handing projects back, make sure that you spend time talking to students about how they can improve them, giving them one focus at least that they could seek to develop the next time.

Subject management issues

Visitors to the classroom

The living artefact – the believer or the religious person – similarly has great potential. A good visitor can be very important for students' being able to really understand the effect of religion on daily lives as well as in the normal religious context. Here are a few suggestions as to how to get the best out of the use of visitors:

1. Meet and talk to the visitor before they visit the class. Get to know them and ask them questions in order to find out what they could offer the class.
2. Explain to the visitor about what is appropriate in a lesson and what is not.

The emphasis is educational, not evangelistic. Encourage them to say things like 'I think' and 'I believe', and not to make statements that demand faith, such as 'You should' or 'You will'. Pressure-to-believe language is not appropriate and must be clearly discouraged.

Case study: Guest speaker

Andrew is part of a team teaching a lesson on Islam with a teacher whose first subject is Geography and has been forced against her good will to teach RE. The Geography teacher is a strict Christian who does not enjoy teaching other faiths. Andrew is worried that she might hi-jack a visit from a Muslim speaker to the school, asking them some difficult or possibly confrontational questions. He is worried that what he perceives as her Islamaphobic views might influence or offend members of the two classes involved.

What can he do to make this situation better? Should he get his Head of Department involved?

If possible, the Head of Department should be at the lesson or they need to talk to the RE teacher in order to make sure that the visitor is treated with the respect that they are entitled to. Visitors need to be aware of what their purpose is – is it always educational, never evangelistic? Similarly, teachers need to realize that RE is not about sharing their faith, but informing others and trying to correct false images of religion that students may have.

1. The lesson before the visit, make sure that students have been pre-briefed about the nature of the visitor. Ask them to write questions that they could ask the visitor.

   Take the questions and sort them through. Remove any that you regard as offensive. Make sure, too, that students' questions are all clear to the visitor – you might need to paraphrase or rephrase them.

2. When the visitor arrives, encourage students to welcome them in a respectful way. Make sure that they maintain this, even if the invited guest says or does something that they may find difficult.

3. If the visitor is doing a presentation, tell students to be quiet and that their questions will be answered after this. Allow supplementary questions if you think that is appropriate. Again, be careful not to allow a student to ask a question that might cause a problem. Know your class!

4. After the lesson, have a debrief with the visitor, asking them whether what they told went well and where things could be improved. Similarly, ask students to write an evaluation of the lesson, asking them especially if there was anything that they did not understand and whether they have any further questions that they now would like to be answered.

Case study: Evangelism in the classroom

Jenny has a guest speaker from a local church to come and talk to her Year 7 students about what it is like to be a Christian today. She had asked her class to prepare a series of questions that they might ask her speaker. When the speaker arrives, they say that they would like to talk about their faith. As they talk, they become increasingly evangelistic, trying to get the pupils to see the errors of their ways.

Many of the class are looking very deeply uncomfortable with what is happening and they are beginning to get restless. What can Jenny do to get the lesson back on the track she wanted without offending her guest speaker?

When you have a guest speaker in, there should be a necessary and obvious respect but this does not mean that things that are against the stated aims of the school or the subject should not be challenged. They should. The issue is how you do so. You might even be able to make a virtue out of it, by allowing students to ask the visitor more substantial questions. A priest can perhaps tell you why a church is built in the shape of a cross, but it is probably a more interesting lesson if you allow them to be questioned about the importance of the cross and why that matters to the Christians.

Organizing trips

The main focus of a trip has to be the re-enforcing or setting the scene for learning in the classroom. Therefore, it is important that they are well planned and appropriate. When planning an RE trip, it is important to do the following:

1. Arrange a visit to the place of worship before you are going to take students there. Is the place really suitable to visit? What problems might bringing a group of students pose?
2. Speak to the leadership of the worship place. Are they prepared for visits from schools? Have they already produced educational resources and, if they have, are they ones that your students could easily use or do you need to adapt/develop them?
3. Does the place of worship require any dress code to be observed by visitors? Are there any other instructions that you need to give so that both students and the members of the religious community are at ease with each other?
4. Ring up the place of worship a week before and make sure that all the arrangements for the visit are understood by both sides.
5. When the students arrive, make sure that you pre-brief them to behave with respect in the place of worship.
6. Think through how far you ask students to take part in acts of worship. Should they bow to the Guru Granth Sahib? Should they join in with the meditation in a Buddhist monastery? How do you encourage them to enjoy the richness of the experience of going to such a place without making them feel that they may compromise or feel uneasy about what they do or because of their personal commitments?

If you think through the issues, then a trip can be a rich experience for all the students involved. If you are only able to take a small cross-section of students, then you can use those who did accompany you to act as peer mentors, reflecting on their experiences. I recently took a group of 30 children from across several classes to a Sikh Gurdwara, which amounted to three or four in the teaching groups. They were able to share their ideas and experiences, which re-enforced the textbooks and the videos that I was using to introduce a project based on the Gurdwara. This made it more relevant to the other members of the groups who had not been able to go. Being educated by your peers can sometimes be more powerful than that which comes from the teacher.

Yet, it should not just be places of worship that should be visited. Museums, both local and national, can provide a vital resource for RE. The British Museum is a superb centre to find many things linked with many of the world's religions. The British Library also has a great collection of sacred books. Yet, as well as the artefacts of a religion that you might find in such museums, think, too, about the other opportunities that museums can bring.

The Imperial War Museum has an excellent range of exhibitions, everything from the Holocaust to the Blitz experience, which can help students to understand war, not just as a discussion, but as a real set of events.

Other museums worth considering a visit include the Natural History Museum or the Science Museum can help in understanding the complexity of the world. You could use it as a way to deepen the debate about the idea of creation and whether it has to be in conflict with modern science.

Institutions like the Commonwealth Institute or the art galleries may also be useful to help students understand the themes that they are studying.

Make sure that you inform students about the appropriate ways to behave in museums.

Cover lessons

When you set cover, there are a few rules of thumb. First, always assume that the person who will be covering is not an RE teacher. Make sure that your instructions are clear so that a non-expert can easily explain to the class. Try to leave a class list for register purposes if this not done as standard in your school/college.

Second, make sure that all the resources – textbooks, work-sheets, exercise books or whatever else – are clearly marked. Sticking a copy of your cover to your desk is good, but also make sure that a colleague near to where you teach has a copy and, if you work in a faculty/team structure, the lead teacher has one, too. Try to put together a kit of all the materials that the lesson needs, so that if anything goes astray, there is another source to photocopy from or get copies to the appropriate room.

Third, set more work to do than you think a class might actually be able to achieve. This will make sure that that if there are some fast finishers of the work you think all should be able to do, then there will be enough for pupils to do.

Fourth, try not to set out the cover in a three-part way. You cannot expect a non-expert to lead a role-play or a discussion, so set tasks that will be straightforward (they don't have to be insultingly easy!).

Fifth, it is probably best to avoid setting a DVD or video, as these can often lead to problems for the member of staff covering and if there is specific religious content, it is best that you are there to help sort out any problems. I once left a Geography colleague of mine with a video about circumcision that turned him white, as he had not anticipated it – and he felt somewhat unable to answer the questions that the class had!

Sixth, make sure that you try to mark any cover work as rigorously as any other piece so that students value the lesson and do not see subsequent cover RE lessons as an opportunity to mess around. Make sure, too, that any misbehaviour is dealt with – colleagues have to know that you are doing your job in a way that shows you value their support.

Always try to type cover – often, handwritten cover is a mess, as people often do it at the last moment. Try to plan your cover a few days in advance, unless it is emergency cover due to illness or an urgent family crisis.

Always make the aim of any cover lesson to make it productive and meaningful for the students as well as making sure that it is as easy as it can be for your colleagues to get on and do administration, marking or anything else that they need to do. They might well be resentful enough about losing their free lesson, so make sure that you ease their pain by carefully planned cover work.

It is quite handy if you have some plastic boxes in which relevant text or exercise books can be placed, with registers and any worksheets or writing paper. If your school does not have a cover sheet, why not have one as shown in the following example.

Period 1	Year 9B. Their exercise books are on the desk. Use the textbooks *Buddhism*, do the tasks on pages 22–23. If they finish these, hand out the sheet on Buddhist marriage. Homework is to complete their project on Buddhist worship. Please collect all exercise books and textbooks and return them to the desk. Please put the note that says 'Period 5' on the exercise books.
Period 2	FREE
Period 3	Year 10 GCSE. The GCSE textbooks are on the desk, together with their files. Please hand these out. Pupils need to read pages 55 to 56 on Christian views of life after death, then, using the writing frame, write an essay on this area. This should be done in silence. All books and textbooks to the desk please. Please put the Period 4 note on the textbooks.
Period 4	Year 11 GCSE. The GCSE textbooks are on the desk, together with their files. Please hand these out. Pupils need to read pages 64 to 65 on Christian views of racism, then, using the writing frame, write an essay on this area. This should be done in silence. All books and textbooks to the desk please. Please put the Period 4 note on the textbooks.
Period 5	Year 9B. Same instructions as Period 1.
THANKS FOR COVERING!	
Any problems, let .... know.	

Lesson observation

There are few teachers who love to be observed, but it is vital to help us raise the standard. It might also be an opportunity to show the importance of the subject to others.

A very secular Deputy Head confided to me that his heart sank when he saw that the topic I was doing was the Christian view of suffering. He was so surprised by the interest and the dynamic I had got going in the class that he kept joining in and asking and responding to my questions. This helped the work of my department enormously!

Yes, I felt I had sweated blood to get that lesson to be the best it could be – but it paid off.

Case study: Lesson observation

Colin's Head of Department undertook a lesson observation 3 days ago but, apart from some very brief feedback at the end of the lesson, he has not had any further feedback. He did not see the Head of Department write down very much on the lesson observation and is concerned that things might have been more negative than he thought, as the HOD seems so reluctant to deal with its results.

What should Colin do?

It is vital that lesson observation feedback is given as soon as possible, so that the person who wrote the notes can transmit their findings while their memory is still fresh and also that of the observed person, so that judgements can be considered and, if necessary, challenged appropriately.

Consider what the following two lesson observations tell you. How would you feel if you received observations like the following examples? How do you think a Head of Department or an observer can communicate what they think without discouraging the person being observed?

Teacher	C Johnson		
Observer	A Billings		
Topic	Jewish Marriage		
Observation time	Period 3	Date	November 8th
Pupil numbers	30	Group	Year 8 (Mixed ability)

Aspect	Standard	Strengths/development points
a) Showing expertise in subject, courses and areas of learning	1	The teacher showed that they had an excellent grasp of the subject, showing that they were able to deepen student knowledge.
b) Planning/sharing and exhibiting clear learning objectives alongside suitable teaching strategies	2	The lesson was well planned and resourced. Lesson objectives were displayed on the board and were referred to by the teacher. These aims were clear and students seemed to understand them.
c) Interesting, encouraging and engaging pupils – maintaining a good pace	2	The lesson got off to a brisk start with an engaging starter, but this was allowed to carry on a little too long, which slowed the pace down and meant that the rest of the lesson plan became less easy to achieve.
d) Challenging pupils and expecting the most from them – promoting equality of opportunity	2	Questioning was well structured so that pupils of all abilities and both sexes were engaged, with many eager to take part in the discussion part of the lesson. Students' ideas were treated with respect and carefully developed by the teacher.
e) Using methods and resources enabling all pupils to learn effectively – differentiation	3	There was a good use of discussion and video to aid some learners. The writing tasks needed writing frames to support pupils with weaker literacy. There needed to be more developed extension tasks for the more able.

Aspect	Standard	Strengths/development points
f) Insisting on high standards of behaviour, using strategies to ensure effective use of time	2	The teacher was quick to deal with any low-level disturbance by pupils and this helped to create a purposeful atmosphere that helped to encourage pupil learning.
g) Making effective use of teaching assistants and other support	2	The teaching assistant was encouraged to help statemented pupils and also contributed to class discussion in a way that helped to develop the lesson.
h) Using homework to reinforce and extend what is learnt in school	1	Homework was set, giving pupils a sheet of questions that encouraged them in independent learning to follow up the theme of this lesson.
i) The use of assessment and AFL strategies to enhance learning and inform planning (e.g., peer/self-assessment, shared criteria, questioning, feedback, target setting)	3	Whilst there was good use of questions, there was little else that could count as AFL. An opportunity to ask pupils to evaluate their and others' answers to written work. The plenary was somewhat rushed and limited in its effectiveness, due to a loss of pace.
j) The quality of pupils' attainment, progress and learning	2	Pupils did learn from this lesson and there was some evidence of progression. Attainment was more difficult to assess, given the shortened plenary at the end of the lesson.

Summary Comments & Targets

This was a well planned lesson on a theme with which the pupils engaged. The starter was good, but was allowed to go on too long, which led to a problem of pace, as you became more conscious of time. There was a good rapport between the class and you but you also need to make sure that this does not again lead to a slowing of the pace.

Whilst there was evidence of pupil progress, an extended plenary might well have helped to develop and test pupils' understanding. You need to think about the needs of the most and least able, which were not always met by this lesson.

You have made a very good start as a teacher here and this lesson confirms that with careful development of the issues highlighted, you should prove to be very successful. Well done!

Overall
Grade: 2

Standards may be graded as: *1 Outstanding, 2 Good, 3 Satisfactory, 4 Inadequate.*

Time	Activity	Comments
11.55	Pupils entered room	They did so calmly and were soon settled by the teacher.
11.57	Starter activity	The lesson objectives were on the board and were shared with the class. This was clear and pupils were engaged quickly with what it was asking them to do.
12.02	Feedback	The groups shared the conclusions from the starter. The teacher handled discussion well, but it was allowed to go on for too long. Perhaps needed prepared questions for pupils to answer?

Time	Activity	Comments
12.17	Video	Teacher explanation and introduction to the video about Jewish marriage. This was clear and concise.
12.22	Reading from textbook	A selection of male/female, strong/weaker readers used in order to read the relevant section.
12.30	Task set about the lesson	Pupils worked quietly on questions from the textbook. There was some differentiation for both weaker and stronger pupils.
12.45	Feedback from the tasks set	Pupils were keen to take part in the feedback
12.51	Plenary	The plenary was well planned but only achieved some of its aims, as the bell went before it was complete. There needs to be a better pace to get to this point with more time to spare.

Teacher	A Johnson
Observer	P Clarke
Topic	Abortion
Observation time	1 hour Date Nov 23rd
Pupil numbers	25 Group Year 10 GCSE

Aspect	Standard	Strengths/development points
a) Showing expertise in subject, courses and areas of learning	3	The teacher did not seem to be on top of the information about the legal situation about abortion, which was a major

Aspect	Standard	Strengths/development points
		part of the lesson. They were uncertain in presenting the different views of Christians about this issue.
b) Planning/sharing and exhibiting clear learning objectives alongside suitable teaching strategies	3	Although written on the board, they were not shared or explained with pupils. This led to a lack of direction in the lesson.
c) Interesting, encouraging and engaging pupils – maintaining a good pace	4	There was too much teacher talk and pupil questions were badly handled and not used as the way to develop learning.
d) Challenging pupils and expecting the most from them – promoting equality of opportunity	3	A minority of pupils dominated class discussion. Not all pupils were on task when the written task was set, which was not addressed by the teacher.
e) Using methods and resources enabling all pupils to learn effectively – differentiation	4	No attempt was made at differentiation, either by input or outcome.
f) Insisting on high standards of behaviour, using strategies to ensure effective use of time	2	Most bad behaviour was challenged but there were many pupils who were chatting when the teacher was talking, which went unchallenged. This disrupted about a quarter of the lesson and led to pupils not achieving as they ought.
g) Making effective use of teaching assistants and other support	3	There was no communication with the teaching assistant to help them.

Aspect	Standard	Strengths/development points
h) Using homework to reinforce and extend what is learnt in school	3	The homework sheet was handwritten and was difficult for many pupils to access. There was insufficient time to talk about it in the depth that it would require in order for pupils to achieve all that they could.
i) The use of assessment and AFL strategies to enhance learning and inform planning (e.g., peer/self-assessment, shared criteria, questioning, feedback, target setting)	4	Whilst the objectives were on the board, they were not shared and there was little attempt to encourage pupils to ask questions beyond a superficial level.
j) The quality of pupils' attainment, progress and learning	4	This was disappointing. Students made little progress during the lesson and there was no effective monitoring of their learning.

Summary Comments & Targets

A potentially interesting lesson, which was weakened by insufficient planning, which led to more teacher talk than was wise. There was a lack of opportunity to develop pupil understanding by assessment for learning. Students were too passive and failed to be engaged in the way that they could have been.

Overall
Grade: 4

Standards may be graded as: *1 Outstanding, 2 Good, 3 Satisfactory, 4 Inadequate.*

Parents' evenings

For the RE teacher, parents' evenings can often present a few challenges. Many parents have a view of the subject that is very outdated and we may have to spend part of our time correcting these false notions. How can we get the best out of these events?
Here are some basic ground rules:

1. Parents mainly want to know if their child is achieving and if they are behaving well. Make sure that in all the talk of levels and the technical language, you remember that parents are not experts (normally!) and will need to have some of this explained to them.

2. Try to start with a positive about a pupil. This will put all at ease, especially if the child is with their parents. Only after the positive, then introduce the issues that need to be addressed, trying to be positive but honest, too. Always have your mark book/assessment information to hand. If you can, have the book or a sample of the students' work there, so that you can reflect on it with the parents to see how they could improve their work. It is important that you can give the parent several pieces of information. How does the child perform in tests? What is their class work like? How capable are they of independent learning through activities such as project or homework? How are they orally? Try to have as much information as possible.

3. Given the frequency of contact in RE, it is always wise to ask who the student is by asking the parent to confirm the time their appointment is. It is easy to forget a child or to give a glowing or not so glowing report by accident to the wrong set of parents about the wrong child!

4. Some parents may well be negative about the subject. What answer will you have to the question 'What's the point of RE?' You will need to have an answer to this question. Use this as an opportunity to reassure them that the purpose is not to brainwash any child into any belief, but to educate them and prepare them for the realities of the multicultural, multi-faith world we live in.

5. Parents will often want to share with you how good/bad their experience of RE was. They also want to tell you about the religious background they have. One mother once proudly told me that her somewhat limited daughter had got high effort marks in RE as 'she has connections'. I asked what exactly these were.

    'Well, I said to her Dad that our June is good at RE due to her grandfather having been a gravedigger.' Try to remain composed at such – I just managed it!

6. Expect some parents to be angered about the content of the subject. I have had parents who have been angered by teaching about capital punishment, which they thought was too liberal. Alternatively, in the post-9/11 world, there can often be a parent who will be quite anti-Islamic. Be prepared for some irrationality from parents, but try to either change the subject or point out the context in which controversial issues are studied – i.e. objectively and not from the point of view of a newspaper editorial (at best) or a pub conversation (at worst).

Case study: Trouble at the parents' evening

Andrew is attending his first parents' evening. He has begun to teach his GCSE group about responses to the issue of capital punishment. In this lesson, he referred to a controversial case that may have involved police corruption leading to what is felt to be an unsafe conviction of someone for murder who was subsequently executed.

Unknown to Andrew, one of his pupils' fathers is a pro-capital punishment campaigner and when his daughter told him about the contents of the lesson, he was very angry and, as it was the day of the parents' evening, he decided to take it up with him personally.

How should Andrew react when the issue comes up? Should he ignore it? Should he get his Head of Department involved? Or should he find a way to use the father's involvement in order to help develop the scheme of lessons?

Andrew needs to be as reasonable as he can, to defuse the situation. If the parent is not satisfied, he should try to involve his Head of Department, asking them to come and talk to the parent. He should also try to keep a note of what is said, if the situation develops.

Working with others – cross-curricular work

It is a good idea to see that teachers do work together and where you can work across departments to extend RE, then do so. Here are some suggestions of things you could do:

1. India week. RE could encourage History and Geography to work with it on a theme week or day about India. Food Technology could add in a 'Taste of India'. The Dance and Drama departments could look at Hindu dance. English could refer to literature that looks at the experience of people who lived in India or were influenced by them.
2. Human rights, human wrongs. RE takes the lead in a week looking at the theme of human rights by putting on an exhibition related to the Holocaust, perhaps of pupil work or the travelling exhibitions that some Jewish groups might supply.
3. Artefact making – work with Technology on making artefacts like mezuzahs or Qu'ran stands.
4. Faith in music. Work with the Music department to look at the music of faiths. You could put on some workshops to look at the different types, from Gospel to the Sikh singing in a Gurdwara or the chanting of monks in either a Roman Catholic or Buddhist monastery.

Other responsibilities in the school

As an RE teacher, there will be times when you will be asked to help the school in collective worship. What is your attitude going to be to that? Think about the following case study and how you might deal with the situation.

Case study: Assembly

Michael has been asked to lead an assembly in the second term of his NQT year. The assembly themes are rigidly set and so it says 'The Resurrection of Jesus' as the topic.

Michael is an agnostic and, while he was flattered to be asked to lead an assembly, he is worried that he will not be able to lead it in a way that the school will find acceptable.

Should he tell someone that he cannot lead the assembly? Should he ask for another theme? Or should he try to find a way that helps him to lead an assembly on this theme without compromising what he believes?

Michael needs to be reassured that no one has to lead an assembly by law, even if they are an RE teacher. There are ways of leading assemblies about the beliefs that you do not share without having to compromise your own belief. However, if he feels a conflict, he needs to say so immediately and let the organizer of assemblies know, so that the problem does not reoccur.

Whilst it is a good thing for a member of staff to be involved in activities like running a sports team or leading the Christian Union, they also need to think through whether there will be any conflict with the other role that they have as a teacher. Ninety-nine times out of 100, it is a good thing for students to see their RE teacher in another context.

RE departmental handbook

A departmental handbook is a necessity for a department to function. This should bring together schemes of work, lessons, policies and school-based information in order to make sure that those who work in the department should (pardon the comment) 'sing from the same hymn sheet'.

What might a departmental handbook look like? The following is an example. This is not meant to be definite and my own is personally developing as school and national policies continue to emerge. You will need to add to this as it goes on.

Religious Education Department Handbook

1. **Personnel in the department**
   The people who teach in the department are
   Bob Johnson, Head of Department. Also in charge of PSHE.
   Karen Robinson NQT
   Paul Heath, Deputy Head.
   The Head of Department regularly meets with members of the department, to encourage reflection on practice, address whole school issues and encourage inset and development.
   The Department also seeks to develop the work of the Humanities Faculty/Team.

2. **Teaching strategies**

   The department tries to teach in a number of different styles, as shown in the scheme of work. Teachers are encouraged to teach in appropriate ways for the students they teach.

   The use of discussion, ICT, research, use of artefacts, visits from members of faith groups as well as the use of textbooks and display work is to be encouraged, amongst other ways to encourage and develop learning. The department is committed to the development of student voice and assessment for learning. Differentiation for all pupils, to help deliver personalized learning is currently being developed.

   The Department follows the County agreed syllabus in Key Stage 3 and the AQA GCSE Syllabus Thinking about God and thinking about morality at Key Stage 4. Non-exam RE pupils in Key Stage 4 follow a reduced version of the GCSE course, though consideration is being given to a certificate of RE.

   The Department seeks to insure that students learn about religion and learn from religion, in line with the model schemes of work. Students are encouraged to reflect with sensitivity and understanding.

3. **Right of withdrawal**

   Parents may exercise their right of withdrawal, by sending a letter to the Head of Department. Arrangements will then be made by the school for withdrawn children to undertake private study.

4. **Spiritual, moral, cultural education**

   RE is very dedicated to providing opportunities for this to happen. The department also works with the PSHE department and the work of the team of people who lead assemblies. The department also contributes to Citizenship by teaching the Citizenship GCSE in parallel with the RE Short course GCSE. The department also seeks to help colleagues in other departments to develop their practice in this area.

5. **Anti-racism, anti-sexism, homophobic and bullying policy**

   The department follows the school policy on racism and sexism (enclosed), homophobia and bullying policies. The department also seeks to insure that all feel included, whatever their background or ability.

6. **Health and safety**
   The Department follows the school's policy in this area. It is important that the classroom is a safe working environment. Members of staff should be good role models of healthy and safety practice.

7. **Collective worship**
   The Head of RE helps to organize the programme of assemblies and has contributed to assemblies. He also has gathered relevant material and worked with the Pastoral Faculty in the development of this part of school life. Members of the Department choose to lead acts of collective worship.

8. **Literacy**
   The department seeks to develop literacy skills via its programme of study. The use of word lists on the module sheets, extended writing, the answering of questions as well as discussion to extend oral skills are important to help in the conceptual development of students. The department is committed to making sure that the language for learning strategy is put into place.

9. **Numeracy**
   Students are encouraged to use and develop their skills in numeracy where relevant to the subject area.

10. **Discipline**
    The teacher in the first instance is responsible but any failure by students to comply must be referred to the Head of Department. Letters home are encouraged where appropriate.
    If the Head of Department cannot address issues with a particular pupil, Heads of House and Faculty will be informed.

11. **Homework**
    Homework should be regularly set and can include writing, research, use of ICT, diagrams, surveys and any other technique that advances the students' learning in the subject. The scheme of work gives suggestions for homework.
    Increasingly, the focus will be on using projects of 3 to 5 home works a term to develop pupils' ability to do extended writing, as the department believes this helps pupils to achieve more than less planned home works.

12. **Differentiation and special needs**
    The department encourages students to develop to their best potential, using differentiation of outcome and input to help them to do so. The work with least able pupils is important, with teachers informed by the SEN department about pupils with special needs.
    The department seeks to extend specially gifted pupils via tasks that develop rather than merely repeat common work. They may also be entered in two separate papers to achieve a full GCSE in Religious Studies.

13. **Scheme of work: included in subsequent pages.** These are written in accordance with the Locally Agreed Syllabus and the Exam syllabus, outlined earlier. It also takes into account the non-statutory guidance given by QCA FOR Key Stage 3 RE.

14. **Tests and exam questions:** included in subsequent pages, together with a section on assessment.

15. **Arrangement for absence:** Teachers are responsible to set their own cover but must leave a copy with the Head of Department as well as in their work area.

16. **Student voice.** The Department is committed to the development of student voice. It regularly seeks to gain insight into student opinions via formal questionnaires and informal feedback. It welcomes the development of student lesson observers, especially in their commitment to help in developing student-friendly approaches to learning.

The role of questioning

The RE teacher needs to develop their ability to draw out information and responses from students in both formal and informal ways. What exactly is questioning? A definition would help us to understand:

Questioning – a classroom technique whose function is to test the extent of pupil's knowledge and understanding to provide pupils with the opportunity to practise oral skills and to promote rapport between teachers and pupils. Judicious use of questioning requires skill and experience especially in teaching languages. If the questions are designed to draw the pupil towards a predetermined conclusion or insight step by step, the technique is known as Socratic questions, a method once favoured in educational circles. (Collins, Downes, Griffiths and Shaw, 1973)

As a definition, it provides a start, but it is limited. Where is the emphasis on questioning as a way to encourage pupils to be critical, to evaluate and achieve the goal of independent learning, not dependent on the input of the teacher?

It also fails to take account of questioning as a skill that involves both literacy and developing oral skills. It also fails because it does not take account of its being not just a classroom activity, but a skill needed by all.

Morgan and Sexton's (1994) definition may help – 'Questions are the chief agent by which meanings are mediated in education.' A clearly asked question may well bring meaning but a badly expressed one will confuse and frustrate. Questions are an important part in mediating meaning, but they are not the only way. Context can convey meaning, even tone of voice.

We need to also think about two styles of questions, making sure that we build them into our lessons:

1. Closed – questions that have a fact that needs to be checked and cannot be varied; for example, 'Who was the founder of Sikhism?' can only be answered by 'Guru Nanak'.
2. Open questions. These allow pupils to show their own response or to realize the difficult nature of reality, such as 'Why do you think Guru Nanak did what he did?' or 'Why do you think there is suffering in the world?'

Bloom's taxonomy and classifying questions

Questioning has been a research area for many writers such Kerry, who has written extensively about the process. He, like many authors, uses Bloom's taxonomy of questions as one of the key ideas in his research. In both the Key Stage 3 strategy documents and the revision booster pack, the Department for Education refers to Bloom's work, by implication making it the standard upon which all development on questioning should take place.

The seven levels in Bloom's model fall into two broad categories:

1. Activities and questions that involve remembering, checking on understanding and applying knowledge – Bloom calls these knowledge, comprehension and application.
2. Activities and questions that involve higher-order critical and creative thinking – Bloom refers to these as analysis, synthesis and evaluation.

Bloom believed questions could be identified as belonging to seven groups. By using this, he believed it would be easier to develop questioning that would lead to greater challenge, taking the teacher away from closed questions that demanded very little of the pupil. For each group, the DfES booklet on questioning gives a minimum of five words or terms that can help to unpack and develop them (DfES, 2004). For example, the questioning skill linked with knowledge could be unlocked by using the words 'define', 'recall', 'describe', 'label', 'identify' and 'match'.

Kerry also groups some questions, suggesting a division by conceptual (about ideas), empirical (about knowledge) and value-related (about the worth/merit of an issue). This is an alternative model to Bloom but, although once favoured by the DfES (for whom Kerry wrote in the 1980s), it no longer is. It is unfortunate that Kerry's approach is not given as a contrast to Bloom, if only for the sake of balance.

Kerry writes 'Given the range and frequency of questions that we ask our pupils, it is curious that few of us attempt to classify the kinds of questions we ask or indeed even to check occasionally how many questions we ask in lesson' (Kerry, 1998). There are five key questions that you can apply to the work you wish pupils to undertake:

What?
Where?
Who?
When?
Why?

These have been used to help pupils to think through issues. Let us look at an example based on the miracles of Jesus:

What – do we mean by a miracle?
Where – in time and in the world are miracles more likely/less likely to take place?
Who – is responsible for the miracle? Can it be explained by the presence of Jesus or another divine being?

When – did it happen? What conditions made it happen? Could they apply to today's world?

Why – did these events happen? Why may they not happen or happen less frequently than in the time of Jesus?

Improving the work of the department

Using action research methods to improve the delivery of RE in school

It is important to reflect on how you can develop the work of the department that you are working in or leading, otherwise problems will not be resolved. One technique that you can use is the action research methods that have become very popular in a number of professions in the last few years.

Action research methods have become very popular amongst university and other parishioners. By actually examining and researching your own situation, you will be able to make some judgements. When I was investigating the topic of how to raise boys' achievement in RE, I chose the following methods of research in order to obtain data that would help my research and would come to influence what was taught in the classroom.

Action research suggests that in order to get an accurate picture of what is going on, you should use a variety of different research methods, as each technique will reveal different but complimentary information.

The following table sets out various approaches I used to try and examine the issue of boys' achievement in Religious Studies GCSE Short Course. I decided to concentrate on using a cross-section of 20 male students to help me.

Research method	Populations	Which pupils/people/resources and why
1. Folders' analysis	20 pupils	Selected to include different perceived abilities
2. Subject-specific questionnaires	20 pupils	Selected across the ability range and from seven different teaching groups

Research method	Populations	Which pupils/people/resources and why
3. General schools questionnaires	20 pupils	Selected across the ability range and from seven different teaching groups
4. Interviews with pupils	12 pupils	Selected from the larger group who did the questionnaire and from groups taught by both myself and my colleague. In tended to reflect diversity of ability
5. Lesson observations	50 pupils	Two classes, one taught by me and one by my colleague
6. Teacher interview	1 teacher	My colleague was selected, as he is the only other member of staff who teaches the cohort under investigation
7. Analysis of textbooks	Three different books	Analysis of the textbooks most used to support the GCSE Short Course
8. Examination of Ofsted reports	Two reports	Used to compare with the inspections undertaken over 20 other schools with my field of study
9. Research journal	Filled in with relevant quotations, draft questionnaires and analysis	This was used throughout the course of the project in order to help develop and refine the questions under examination
10. Literature review		This was used to help develop the research focus and to test the interpretations emerging from the data in order to develop the research focus

I asked my colleague to give me his detailed reflection on the questionnaires in order to contrast with my reflections. I asked him to do this on paper so that I did not give him any hints as to my own personal reflections on the data obtained.

The examination of other sources of data, such as textbooks and the Ofsted reports, were used in order to help me get a fuller picture of the context within which the research was being undertaken.

There were to be limits to my methods. If I had been able to survey a wider number of pupils, there could have been different results. On balance, I think that the questionnaires used were effective, especially as they had combinations of different styles of questions. Using both a subject-focused and a general school questionnaire provided me with information that might not have become obvious and would have led the research in another direction.

There could have been a greater exploration of both textbooks and alternative, existing syllabus options.

Interviewing could have been more extensive but I do feel that I was able to let the pupils speak in such a way that I did not lead them to ideas or conclusions that I was making. Inevitably, a study focused on 20 children and on two teachers is limited but, despite this, the data obtained did help me to consider the area of male attainment in RE. There is a limited amount of literature that is directly on this subject and had there been more available, it may well have led my study into other areas.

Any teacher using action research will be able to test theories and ideas within a class setting, being able to use reflection on existing practice as well as test strategies to help with improvement of teaching and learning. It also enables a teacher to make an input into the research community as well as helping to develop good practice and understanding in the profession.

Is it therefore possible to develop boy-friendly RE? On the basis of my action research, I came to the following conclusions: not all of these could I put into action, given that some of them are about the way examination boards behaved. However, it has informed my planning of topics and how I teach them. There are a number of ideas that have come out of the research that suggest ways in which to make the subject more appealing and relevant to males.

Any curriculum or syllabus revision will also hopefully make the subject more inviting or relevant to all pupils, not just one sex. My reading and research suggest that gender is constantly to some degree being redefined, making this area difficult to draw lines between two circumscribed genders of 'male' and 'female' – so both may well benefit:

1. We need to reflect on the existing syllabus and teaching styles. The research suggests that males are not necessarily hostile to RE but there are topics in existing syllabuses that we need to try to teach in a way that is inclusive of males as well as females. Take, for example, the issue of abortion. The questions in textbooks and in examination papers do not appear to obviously involve males: the moral debates are often narrowed down to the choice of the woman or the teachings of the religion.

   Very little attention is given to the male's involvement in conception and the possible decision to have an abortion. It seems that the syllabus re-enforces one of the views of our culture that it is ultimately a woman's choice. Clearly, within many faith traditions, the role of fatherhood and the importance of the family are a religious and social unit. If we were to include this approach, would that help males to connect more with the topic?

   Similarly, in the issue of divorce, we could use Fathers for Justice as a case study in why this issue affects or potentially affects young men.

   We also must realize that gender is an ongoing, developing concept that has no totally fixed point, so we must try to address this so that pupils who may come from backgrounds that stress rigid definitions of male and female roles can be prepared for the world as it is becoming, rather than as the culture might suggest.

2. We should consider changing the syllabus to reflect male concerns. Blaylock's suggestion that areas like the ethics of sport and pornography may well engage males may help. They may also engage some females who have culturally become more 'laddish' in their attitudes and culture. Are there other areas that may well also connect with men? In the existing syllabus, issues of science and war have often seemed to be areas that have engaged males in the way that topics such as marriage have not. However, we should consider our teaching so that we avoid adopting a stereotypical view of maleness or limit the curriculum to what we perceive to be more acceptable to males.

   Any change of syllabus should help to develop and engage with the Religious Education of both sexes, as the models of male and female interests are in a state of flux as the perceived identities attached to gender are seen to be in a time of transition by the pupils who have identified within their own group a sense of identity in crisis (the need to be macho was identified by some of the interviewees as a key theme).

3. The use and the design of textbooks. On my own examination of the textbooks currently being used in my department and the responses of the interviewees, there is a perceived lack in these of text and illustration that can engage with males.

Serious thought needs to be given by examination boards, textbook publishers and writers to designing and writing material that can be accessed in a way that, while including female experience, also addresses maleness.

There has rightly been a great deal of work done to reduce sexism against females in textbooks, but now it would seem that we should consider developing a critical awareness of the needs of males to avoid to changing one sexism for another.

This suggests some detailed consideration in order to avoid the development of new or the rekindling of old stereotypes. It may be that the use of interactive whiteboards with CD-ROMs and other programs that may be more readily available than textbook material for this purpose, as books, by their nature, take longer to produce and cannot be responsive to change as quickly as electronically produced material.

4. From the initial sampling of pupils' work in the classes that I teach, there does seem to be a strong correlation between raising male achievement by the use of word processing – something that Ofsted (Ofsted, 2003) have also noted in their research about male achievement. This inevitably raises acute problems about the availability of computers to help pupils to raise their standards. Could we raise pupil attainment in the final exam by making sure that it would be online? It is likely that more examinations could be taken in this way in future but I suspect that, as with most developments, RE would be the last subject to benefit from such a change. This would require most schools to encourage the greater development of ICT than is currently available. This would remove problems associated with male handwriting, which often lacks the confidence and legibility of female pupils.

5. Those boys who least achieve in Religious Education are those who are not necessarily those who lack a personal encounter with religion but they do seem to be marked with especially deep-seated problems with literacy. A greater emphasis on literacy across the curriculum may have the effect of raising pupil achievement in a subject that demands many literacy skills as well as an ability or empathy to thinking metaphorically.

6. The use of pupil input in shaping the curriculum. Using the approach of Friere and Rogers suggests the need to adopt a greater dialogue about the issues that they think are important and to listen to them in what they think will aid their learning. My interviewees had some ideas for topics that they thought should be included in a syllabus. With syllabus revisions in the subject due in 2008, it would be helpful if examination boards did some research of pupils' interests alongside the views of teachers or the faith communities to inform this process.

7. The use of an oral in GCSE Short Course RE accreditation. In English GCSE, there is an oral examination that seeks to assess the discussion skills in the subject, which gives pupils 10 per cent of their final grade. RE requires many of the same skills that are found in English oral tests: the ability to formulate and express an argument. Many boys whom I surveyed especially appreciated RE as a subject that they could discuss and my experience of teaching suggests that many are much more confident when discussing than writing answers to questions. If RE GCSE were able to allocate 10 per cent of its final mark on the basis of an oral, this may help to raise achievement with boys who might struggle with written coursework in other subjects and the examination paper in RE.

However, this would require some consideration, as the practicalities of arranging orals for a year cohort when they most likely only have 1 hour a week would be difficult, especially as many schools are increasingly opting to put an entire cohort through the examination. One solution could be to reduce the content of the syllabuses of the GCSE RE Short Course in order to allow this innovation to be developed.

Could pupils be involved in drawing up the content of the suggested GCSE oral component, with some guidance from the examination boards to ensure a common standard nationally? There then becomes a question of the assessment and the setting of the universal standard.

What might seem an acceptable standard of speaking in one culture may be perceived to be less than acceptable within another school context. The danger could be that we are essentially teaching pupils to speak in one particular way rather than encouraging them to speak in a coherent and individual way about the issues raised by the subject.

Any improvement in the teaching of RE aimed at boys will, if effective, I would suggest, have consequences for the girls and their experiences of the subject every bit as much as the experiences of boys. From my research and reading, there seem to be varieties of masculinities amongst the boys I teach. This needs to be addressed when teaching.

My project also suggests a perceived problem of the feminization of the curriculum that needs to be addressed to give balance. From my reading and experience, there also should be some appreciation of a wider variety of femininities that are present, many of which are increasingly including characteristics that were once seen as male, often characterized at its extremes as 'laddette' behaviour.

With this realization and the other issues raised in this research, hopefully, this will lead to a balanced curriculum that will appeal to both genders.

Monitoring

Monitoring is essential to help raise achievement in any department. Amongst the areas that need to be monitored and reported on are:

1. Lessons – formal and informal lesson observations are essential.
2. Sampling of class, home and exam papers. It is important that you work together as a department to make sure that any mark schemes are enforced in similar ways. This will also help you to think about the summative and formative comments you make on pupils' work.
3. Interviewing selected pupils. This can be useful in providing good feedback – see the section on action research.
4. Surveys – if you make these anonymously, you may be able to get information that is of great value.
5. Student lesson observers – with guidance, they can provide useful insight into what pupils experience.
6. Exam analysis – this, too, should help to gain knowledge of how effective teaching and learning are at Key Stage 4.
7. Comparing levels – what are the levels like for individual pupils in subjects that are broadly comparable? History and English are fairly close parallels in terms of the skills that you need to develop as well as in teaching approaches.

The greater variety of approaches used will help to make sure that there is a realistic view of the work of the department and the school context in which it operates.

Local networking with other RE teachers

Developing local networks with other RE teachers is highly beneficial, as you cannot necessarily rely on being given time to attend all the Inset you would like to attend.

Getting to know and work with a group of colleagues – my suggestion would be in four to six local schools – can help you to share ideas and teaching strategies with each other. This is vital for RE teachers, as we will often be in one or two-people departments. Just meeting others and realizing that they are having the same issues as you are faced with can be a great release from stress. With many local authorities unable to provide the advisory support, this is becoming increasingly important. Peer help is sometimes of more use than experts', as you know it has been tried and tested by the fire of the classroom!

National networking with RE teachers

There are many organizations that seek to help to develop the work of RE teachers. NATRE (The National Association for the Teachers of RE) seeks to help and support teachers through publications like *RE Today* (a magazine that has lesson ideas, news of developments in RE nationally as well as a review of resources and books) and training events across the country. They regularly produce booklets crammed full of lesson ideas and resources.

They also, in connection with CEM, produce an excellent set of resources themselves, including videos and booklets. They can be contacted via their website at www.retoday.org.uk. There are currently over 2,500 teachers benefiting from being members of NATRE. NATRE also works across the different sectors of education – primary, secondary and those in higher education are all represented on its governing committee.

Another organization that seeks to help RE teachers is the Farmington Trust, based in Harris Manchester College, Oxford. This will fund sabbatical terms for RE teachers and has an excellent website full of previous reports by former fellows. You can get in contact with me at www.farmington.ac.uk. They will also fund people to undertake research. Fellows attend a yearly conference where good practice is shared and new ideas are discussed. They will also fund some research projects that are school-based and are keen to help sponsor meetings of Farmington fellows who live near each other and wish to network with each other.

The St Gabriel's weekends also give a yearly opportunity for those newly qualified or within a few years of qualifying as teachers, with many key players in RE leading seminars and teaching sessions to help.

See Chapter 10 for other useful contacts and also *100 Ideas for Teaching Religious Education* (Continuum, 2008).

Pupils' career opportunities with Religious Education

'What use is RE to me? I don't want to be a nun/monk/priest/pope?' Many pupils may say this to you when you are doing an options evening. Here is a list of some possible career paths that they might choose with a qualification in RE/RS. It is important for students to realize that RE is a subject that can help them to develop understandings and skills that can be of use to them in a variety of jobs and professions. These include:

- administrator
- advice worker
- counsellor
- doctor
- housing adviser
- journalist
- lawyer
- lecturer
- librarian
- minister of religion
- politician
- psychologist
- social worker
- teacher
- youth and community worker

Skills developed when studying Religious Education

The ability to say a prayer or know where things are in the Bible is not the prime concern of RE. As part of a good general education, it should enable students to develop the following skills:

- clear and logical thinking
- critical evaluation
- empathy
- interest in moral, social and political ideas
- literacy and expression
- negotiating
- organizing
- planning
- problem solving
- research
- understanding different ideas and people
- working to deadlines
- working with others, especially with different backgrounds and beliefs from our own

It is important that when we are designing lessons, we should give students the opportunity to practise these skills. When students begin to see that the skills they are being taught in role-plays, for example, could help them when they go for an interview or help them when trying to argue their case in a job, they may well think more highly of them.

Collecting resources for an RE department

Videos/DVDs useful for the RE teacher

As a rule of thumb, try to avoid any film or DVD shot in black and white, as many students are resistant to this. When choosing a film, make sure that you have seen it all the way through – you might need to edit it for appropriateness. Be aware of the film's certification. Keep your eye out for newer films that might explain similar topics.

Also, just because a film does not have an overt religious theme or input, don't reject it – it may help to build a bridge with students, as it might highlight moral and spiritual issues. You don't always have to go for the Biblical epic to make students think about a topic relevant to RE.

It is very important that you should also develop worksheets or other extension work from the videos, so that students do not see them as a time-wasting exercise or as a way of the teacher having some time off, marking written work.

Here is a selection of some tried and tested favourites that normally provoke good reactions with classes. You might like to survey students, as they might have suggestions that they might like you to be aware of:

Bend It Like Beckham (cert. 12, 2002) The British-made comedy that looks at sexism, being a Sikh in a multicultural society, racism and football.

Blood Diamond (cert. 15, 2007) Powerful film about corruption and materialism about the Third World.

Cry Freedom (1987) Powerful film about racism, following the story of South African activist Steve Bike and his friendship with newspaper editor Donald Woods.

Dead Man Walking (1995) Powerful film about capital punishment and the work of Sister Helen Preteen.

Flatliners (cert. 15, 2000) Medical students set out to prove that there is a life beyond death. Warning – contains late 1980s big hair!

Gandhi (cert. U, 1982) Classic study of the Indian campaigner and Hindu leader.

Let Him Have It (cert. 15, 1991) The story of Derek Bentley, hanged for an involvement in a robbery that led to murder, even though he did not do the crime. Raises issues of justice and the debate about capital punishment.

The Lion, the Witch and the Wardrobe (cert. U, 2005) The re-telling of C.S. Lewis' classic tale will be useful for looking at symbolism and allegory, especially focusing on Aslan as a symbol of Christ.

The Lord of the Rings trilogy (2001–03) There are many vivid images and parts of the story that could be applied to religion, such as Frodo's struggle with the Ring.

Little Buddha (cert. PG, 1993) A contemporary search for a reincarnated Buddhist teacher is set against some flashbacks to the original Buddha, which are excellent for the teaching of Buddhism. The modern part of the film is best avoided!

Malcolm X (1992) Spike Lee's epic re-telling of Malcolm X: I would use selected parts of this, the most important being the Hajj Malcolm made to Makkah and the way it changed his thinking about race.

The Matrix (cert. 15, 2000) Science-fiction blockbuster with Keanu Reeves that raises questions about reality, what being human means and the struggle to find truth in the world. Does this help teaching the idea of Plato's cave, Zen Buddhism and other religious ideas? Many think it will!

The Miracle Maker (cert. U, 2000) An animated life of Jesus, featuring an all-star cast including Ralph Fiennes as Christ.

My Left Foot (1988) The story of Christy Brown, the author who battled against prejudice against his disability in twentieth-century Ireland.

The Nativity (cert. PG, 2006) A re-telling of the birth of Jesus. The second half of the film is especially good, the first a little slow. This will help students to see behind the Christmas-card pleasantness to understand the political and social issues of the time.

The Passion (2008) The excellent BBC/HBO production tracing the last 7 days of the life of Jesus. The episode of the

Resurrection presents an interesting new take on why the disciples did not recognize Jesus!

Prince Caspian (2008) Another of Lewis' Narnian chronicles that will raise questions about Creation and fighting for a good cause.

The Prince of Egypt (cert. U, 1998) A superb cartoon re-telling of the Moses story, this features songs and raises many questions about the plagues and the Passover.

Rain Man (cert. 15, 1988) The Oscar-winning film on autism can be used with older students to help them to reflect on disability, as Tom Cruise discovers his long-lost autistic brother (played by Dustin Hoffman).

Shadowlands (cert. 15, 1994) The story of C.S. Lewis and his love for Joy Gresham. It explores the themes of suffering and God's purposes. Previewing is essential, as it frankly examines death and grief in a way that some students might not be used to.

The Simpsons Movie (cert. U, 2007) Looks at environmental issues in a student-friendly way!

The Simpsons – Heaven and Hell (cert. U, 1998) A selection of four episodes that all have spiritual themes, like heaven, hell, heresy and evil.

The Boy in the Striped Pyjamas (cert. U, 2008) A powerful and disturbing story of a child whose father is in charge of a concentration camp and the Jewish friend he makes there.

The Short Life of Anne Frank (cert. E, 2003) A superb 28-minute documentary about the life of Anne Frank, sold at the Anne Frank house and available online at www.annefrank.nl. There are other film versions of the story.

The Truman Show (cert. 12, 1999) The film about a man caught up in the ultimate reality programme in which only he isn't an actor. This could be used as a modern compare/contrast with the story of Prince Siddhartha.

The Vicar of Dibley (cert. 12, BBC, 2007) The first episode in Series One would form a good basis for a discussion about sexism and the role of women priests.

Remember to use the BBC website to see what DVDs for the subject are available. If you can find copies of the *Testament* series of DVDs produced by the Bible Society and the BBC in the 1990s, these are excellent resources, as they re-tell Biblical stories including those of Abraham, Moses, Ruth and Elijah.

Choose carefully – the days when a class would just be quiet by the magic of the video are long gone!

Music that could be useful for the RE teacher

Following is a selection of music that might be good to use to illustrate various themes:

Jesus Christ Superstar and *Godspell* will give students the Jesus story in a way that uses the form of musicals.

Handel's *Messiah* and Bach's *St Matthew's Passion* might also be useful.

Fiddler on the Roof might well be useful to illustrate Judaism.

The work of Yusuf Islam might be used to show the influence of Islam on an artist.

There are various CDs of Gregorian or Buddhist chanting that might be useful.

An appropriate 'chill-out' CD might also be useful to calm classes for a mediation or stilling exercise.

A library – try to develop a lending library of religious books, especially biographies, that students can take away at their leisure.

The internet – keep an eye out for websites and a visit to 'You Tube' will be well worth it if you are looking for material.

Resources/addresses/websites for the RE teacher

Artefacts

One of the best places to find artefacts is Articles of Faith Ltd. They can be contacted at Articles of Faith Ltd, Resource House, Kay Street, Bury BL9 6BU; tel. 0161 763 6232 or 0161 763 5366; email faith@resourcehouse.co.uk; website www.articlesoffaith. co.uk.

They publish an extensive catalogue that also includes a calendar of the key festivals in the religions of the world. Every department needs a copy!

Christianity resources

Catholic Truth Society, 38–40 Eccleston Square, London SW1Y 1PD

Quakers (The Religious Society of Friends), Friends House, Euston Road, London NW1 2BJ

Church of England Board of Social Responsibility, Church House, Dean's Yard, London SW1P 2NZ

The Methodist Church, www.methodist.org.uk

The United Reform Church, www.urc.com

The British Orthodox Church, www.britishorthodox.org

Lourdes website, www.lourdes-france.com – a vital resource if pupils are looking at miracle stories

Worth Abbey's website, www.worthabbey.com – may give pupils an insight into life in the monastery

The Lord's Day Observance Society, www.lordsday.co.uk – will help pupils to understand why Christians see Sunday as special

Association of Christian Teachers, 94a London Road, St Albans, Hertfordhsire AL1 1NX; email act@christians-in-education. org.uk.

The Christian Muslim Forum, Ludgate House, 107–111 Fleet Street, London EC4A 2AB; website www.christianmuslim forum.org. This organization is designed to bring Christians and Muslims together on various projects, including reflecting on education

Three Faiths Forum, Star House, 104 Grafton Road, London NW5 4BA. This seeks to bring together Jews, Christians and Muslims

Judaic resources

Board of Deputies, www.bod.org.uk

Agency for Jewish Education, www.aje.org.uk – a source of information about the Jewish faith

The Holocaust Centre, Laxton, Newark, Notts NG22 0PA, tel. +44 (0) 1623 836627, fax +44 (0) 1623 836647, email office@ bethshalom.com

Yad Vashem, the Holocaust museum in Jerusalem, http://yad-vashem.org.il, www.annefrank.org – an excellent resource with Anne Frank-relevant information

Islamic resources

The Regent's Park Mosque can be visited in central London. It can be contacted at www.islamicculturalcentre.co.uk

One of the best sites on the web for Islam material is

www.realislam.com and www.bbc.co.uk.religion/religions/islam/

If you were researching art in Islam, then try http://bmag.org.uk/artislam, which has many pictures of interest

One key organization is the Muslim Council, MCB, PO Box 57330, London E1 2WJ, email admin@mcb.org.uk

The Muslim Teachers' Association, c/o m.matharoo@plashet.-newnham.sch.uk

Islam and Citizenship, School Development Support Agency, Alliance House, 6 Bishop Street, Leicester, tel. 0116 299 5939, email khalid.mahmood@sdsa.net

Hindu resources

www.hinduwebsite.com

www.hinducounciluk.org

BAPS Shri Swaminarayan Mandir, 105–119 Brentfield Road, Neasden, London NW10 8LD, tel. (+44-20) 8965 2651, fax (+44-20) 8965 6313, email info@mandir.org

Another possible contact is www.iskcon.org.uk, the website of the International Society for Khrisna Consciousness. Visit www.iskcon-london.org to get information about visiting their temple in London

Buddhist resources

The very best site on the web is www.buddhanet.net

Other good sites include www.lbc.org.uk, which belongs to the London Buddhist Centre

Another good one is http://bentrem.sycks.net, which has many connections

There are many Buddhist monasteries that can be contacted. One of the best prepared for visitors is on the edge of Chichester in West Sussex – Cittaviveka, Chithurst Buddhist Monastery, Chithurst (W. Sussex), Petersfield, Hampshire GU31 5EU, tel. +44 (0)1730 814 986, fax +44 (0)1730 817 334. For enquiries about visiting Cittaviveka, please write directly to the address above. Chithurst Buddhist Monastery does not operate a public email address. Office hours to contact for a visit: Mon, Wed and Sat, 07.00–08.00 a.m.; Tue and Thu, 10.00 a.m.–12.00 p.m.

Please note that many monasteries have retreats, which means that visiting during these periods is not allowed.

Sikhism resources

www.sikh.org – a major source of information about the Sikh faith

www.bbc.co.uk/religion/religions/sikhism/ – a good basic introduction to the faith

www.srigurugranthsahib.org – this site includes material from the Sikh holy writings, the Guru Granth Sahib

www.sikhiwiki.org – a Sikh Wikipedia that looks at all the topics of importance to Sikh believers

One valuable place for resources has to be the Sikh Missionary society, who can be contacted at Sikh Missionary Society UK, 10 Featherstone Road, Southall, Middlesex UB2 5AA, tel. 020 8574 1902, email info@sikhmissionarysociety.org

Other faith resources

The Bahais, www.bahai.org – the official site of the Bahais, which is full in detail

Jainism, www.iamjain.org – a good site that explains what is like to be a Jain today

Shinto, www.bbc.co.uk/religion/religions/shinto/ – a very good, straightforward account of the religion

Confucianism, www.religioustolerance/org/confucianism – a very accessible site that gives a good account of the Chinese religion

Rastafarianism, www.bbc.co.uk/religion/religions/rastafari/ – will give you the basic facts of the religion. You can also use rastafarionline.com as well as sites dedicated to Bob Marley

Atheist/agnostic information, British Humanist Association, 1 Gower Street, London WC1E 6HD, tel. 020 7079 3580, fax 020 7079 3588, email www.humanism.org.uk

Moral and spiritual issues resources

Development and poverty issues

Christian Aid, PO Box 100, London SE1 7RT, www.christianaid.org

Tear Fund, 100 Church Road, Teddington TW11 8QE, www.tearfund.org

CAFOD, Romero Close, London SW9 9TY, www.cafod.org

www.islamic-relief.com – one of the main Muslim development charities

www.tzedek.org.uk – a Jewish organization, which can also be contacted at Tzedek, c/o 61 Llanvanor Road, London NW2 2AR

www.hinduaid.org

www.unitedsikhs.org

www.karunatrust.org – a Buddhist development charity, which can also be contacted at Karuna Trust, 72 Holloway Road, London

www.oxfam.org.uk

www.dfid.gov.uk – DFID produce booklets on development themes as well as a magazine called *Developments*

War and peace issues

Christian CND, Mordechai Vanunu House, 162 Holloway Road, London N7 8DQ, www.ccnd.gn.apc.org

www.anglicanpeacemaker.org.uk – a Church of England group committed to pacifism

www.peacemakers.tv – designed to question stereotypes and overcome divisions in society

www.baptist-peace.org.uk

Campaign against the Arms trade (Christian network), www.caat.org.uk/getinvolved/Christian

www.paxchristi.org.uk – the leading Roman Catholic peace organization

Animal welfare issues

www.rspca.org.uk – the site of the RSPCA, who have an extensive number of materials for teaching animal welfare. Also useful are the Friends of the Earth at www.foe.co.uk and Greenpeace at www.greenpeace.org.uk. There are many other groups, but be cautious about the ones that you point pupils towards

The International Fund for Animal Welfare can be contacted at IFAW, Free post SEA 13616, Rochester ME1 1BR

Vegetarian websites

www.in-site.co.uk is an excellent site, as it lists the Top 50 vegetarian sites

Religious sites looking at animal issues

A Rocha is an international conservation charity with a Christian basis that can be contacted at international@arocha.org

Sanctity-of-life issues

Abortion-related sites
All of these sites need to be viewed and, if used in school, there may be a need to load them onto an intranet rather than allow open access.

www.lifecharity.org.uk – the major anti-abortion campaign
www.catholic-ew.org.uk – the Roman Catholic Church's teaching on abortion explained
www.christiananswers.net – seeks to answer many questions
www.abortionrights.org.uk – the best pro-choice site for information

Cloning
www.ornl.gov – information about cloning and the human genome project

Human rights issues

Christian Solidarity Worldwide, www.csw.org.uk – campaign on behalf of Christians being persecuted
www.prejean.org – website of Sister Helen Prejean, who campaigns against capital punishment
Amnesty International has an extensive site at www.amnesty.org

Other faiths, too, are interested in human rights issues; see, for example:

Islamic Human Rights Commission, www.ihrc.org
Buddhist views on human rights, www.buddhanetz.org
Hindu Human Rights, www.hinduhumanrights.org

Afterword

Jim Wallis, the American activist and preacher, points out that the best teachers are those who commit themselves to continue to learn.

We need to make sure that we model this in the way we conduct ourselves. We need to keep ourselves up to date with the religious and ethical debates within which we find ourselves. When we show that we value continuing the development of knowledge to students, they will see the importance of life-long learning.

We also need to encourage students to understand the difference between knowledge and wisdom. Knowledge is the gaining of facts: with wisdom, we use those facts with an understanding of who we are and the need to think and feel about other people. We do not want to be like Mr Gradgrind in Dickens' *Hard Times*, who can classify everything but does not have any warmth or empathy to understand what he has learnt.

RE should encourage students to question, to think and to make their own commitments to truth, however they understand that word. What a privilege we have to share the great ideas, stories and people of faith with young people. Do not take it for granted.

Can one teacher of RE make a difference? Absolutely. It can be you and it can be me!

Let us try to change the world, one pupil at a time.